WHAT ABOUT Heaven and Hell?

WHAT ABOUT
Heaven & Hell?

Douglas J. Rumford

TYNDALE HOUSE PUBLISHERS, INC. | WHEATON, ILLINOIS

Library of Congress Cataloging-in-Publication Data

Rumford, Douglas J.
   What about heaven and hell? / Douglas J. Rumford.
      p. cm.
   Includes bibliographical references.
   ISBN 0-8423-7405-1 (pbk.)
   1. Heaven—Christianity.   2. Hell—Chrsitianity.   I. Title.

BT846.2R862000
236'.24—dc21   99-086460

Printed in the United States of America

06   05   04   03   02   01   00
7   6   5   4   3   2   1

CONTENTS

CHAPTER ONE

"I'm Not Sure I Believe in All That Stuff about Heaven and Hell"

"It's really wonderful of you to come, but I need to tell you right up front that I don't really believe in all that stuff about heaven and hell, the Bible, and Jesus."

Ann said these words to me within minutes of our meeting for the first time. She had recently been diagnosed with cancer, and her neighbors, members of my congregation, had asked her if she'd like me to visit her. She said yes and, through her directness and candor, opened the door to one of the most honest, heartsearching explorations of faith I've ever witnessed.

"They say it's really bad," she said softly, motioning me to a chair in her sun-drenched family room. "I'm not really sure what to do."

In her midfifties, Ann was enjoying life with her husband. They had been eagerly anticipating his early retirement and the opportunities for travel that it would bring. Now the doctor's report had come like a sudden, violent thunderstorm on what had been a beautiful, balmy day.

"I must stay strong for my husband," Ann said, her voice breaking. "He can't stand to see someone sick. I can't show my pain. I can't break down. I must be strong. I must!"

Her intensity was deeply moving. As our conversation turned to God, she softened a bit, exposing her anguished hope. "I do try to pray," she admitted, "but I don't feel like God is listening. I really don't know what to ask of him, except for strength to get through this."

Ann believed that death is final, that there is no afterlife. "Before, it was a theory," she said, "a topic of conversation. But now that I'm staring death in the face . . ." Her voice drifted off as her eyes filled with tears.

The subject of heaven and hell is not just an arcane question for theologians and philosophers. It is a matter of urgent importance for every one of us. Each of us will one day face death. While to some it may seem far off, it will come for all of us—a fact that Philip, father of Alexander the Great, was determined to keep before him. Every morning Philip was awakened by a servant who said, "Philip, remember you must die."[1]

My dad, who was in life-insurance sales, found people resistant to facing the fact that they would die. "Some of the salesmen would say, 'If you die . . .' but I had to lovingly and firmly say, 'Now *when* you die, how would you hope your loved ones will be cared for?'" recalled Dad.

Not only will we die, we will also be confronted with death many times in our life: family members, friends, celebrities, and leaders will die within our lifetime. What we believe deep within our heart will make all the difference in how we cope with the reality of death.

Is there an afterlife? If so, what is it like? Are there really two possible destinations? Will the actions of this life affect us in the next life? How can we be sure where we will go? This book considers what the Bible teaches about life after death, about heaven and hell. Now some people may think it's impractical to study heaven and hell. How can we worry about heaven and hell when a nation is in moral crisis, or a student is struggling in school, or a breadwinner fears losing a job, or a relationship is on the rocks? How could the reality of heaven and hell possibly be relevant? Stay with me. We will see that the most important factor in determining the quality of *now* is understanding what will happen *then*.

YOUR DESTINATION REALLY MATTERS!

When traveling, your desired destination determines all of your planning. You wouldn't pack Bermuda shorts for a visit to Alaska in the winter or a down parka for a jaunt to Cancun in the summer. If you're going to visit a foreign country, you might want to study the native language or at least bring along a dictionary and phrase book. If you're going to the Caribbean, you wouldn't plan for any snow skiing. On the other hand, a trip to the mountains of Colorado in winter probably wouldn't involve any sunbathing at the beach. Some destinations may require physical conditioning. When I was preparing to go kayaking on the Sea of Cortéz, off the coast of Baja California, I prepared with some moderate exercises so I could enjoy the experience. Again, your desired destination determines your planning.

The same principle applies to major life goals. Where do you want to go in life? Think about planning for a career. If you want to be a doctor, you have to have good grades in high school, get a bachelor's degree, and then go to medical school. Then you have to complete a residency and medical-board examinations. A career destination in medicine will govern where you live and may determine your decisions about marriage and family planning.

What about your *final* destination? And I'm not talking about retirement. What about your final destination in life? Have you thought about it? Has your desired destination shaped your thinking?

A number of the high school youth from our church were shaken recently when a high school senior was killed on a Sunday morning on her way home from another church. A car had run a red light and hit her vehicle broadside. Ashley had been a strong Christian, and her memorial service was a powerful testimony of faith and hope. But too many of us are spiritually unprepared for sudden death.

We don't know when our final moment on this earth will arrive. Most of us don't think about it, don't plan for it, and don't take it seriously.

What kinds of plans have you made?

WHAT IF THIS WORLD IS ALL THERE IS?

Sarah Winchester's husband had accumulated a vast fortune by manufacturing and selling rifles. After he died of influenza in 1918, she moved to San Jose, California. In her grief, Sarah pursued her interest in spiritualism. When she sought out a medium to contact her dead husband, the medium told her, "As long as you keep building your home, you will never face death."

Sarah believed the medium. She purchased an unfinished seventeen-room mansion and started expanding it. The construction project continued until she died at the age of eighty-five. It cost five million dollars at a time when workmen earned fifty cents a day. The mansion had grown to one hundred fifty rooms, thirteen bathrooms, two thousand doors, forty-seven fireplaces, and ten thousand windows. It contained stairways that led nowhere and doors that opened into walls. When construction stopped at her death, enough materials remained to have continued building for another eighty years!

The writer of Hebrews speaks of "those who through fear of death were subject to lifelong bondage" (Hebrews 2:15, RSV). Today, Winchester House stands as more than a tourist attraction. It is a silent witness to the dread of death that holds millions of people in bondage. While Sarah Winchester may be an extreme example, she was one of many people who construct complicated systems to avoid facing the reality of the human condition.[2]

Your destination not only determines your plans, it shapes your responses to all of life. If you believe that there's nothing more to life than what you are experiencing right now—that when the casket closes it's all over—your belief will affect every decision you make.

If this life is all there is, it's difficult to find comfort and courage in the midst of stress and pain. There's no hope at the bedside of one who is about to die. There's little purpose in living life heroically. If earth is the final destination, you're going to need to develop some very interesting coping strategies. How can you make sense of a life that, quite literally, dead-ends?

WHY IS IT HARD TO BELIEVE IN HEAVEN?

Ann saw herself as someone who had "moved beyond" the primitive superstitions of earlier generations. "I've always been a delving, questioning person," she explained. "How can I accept what the Bible says about death when I don't believe what it says about Creation and evolution?" As her conversation proceeded, however, Ann gave another reason for her skepticism. "The concept of eternal life is beyond my wildest imagination," she said. "I just can't bring myself to believe in it." Ann's skepticism is not unusual. Many people in modern society find it hard to believe in heaven.

IT'S HARD TO BELIEVE IN HEAVEN BECAUSE WE LIVE IN A SKEPTICAL AGE

An antisupernatural bias has gripped our minds. Science has eclipsed theology in explaining the nature of life. The industrial revolution has brought greater prosperity and an emphasis on materialism. Belief in heaven is written off as primitive, wishful thinking. And yet, even skeptics find themselves wondering. Deep within us, above and beyond our human logical systems, there is a longing that won't let go.

There are times in life when we are forced to think of the big picture. It may be as we stand beside the bed of one laboring to catch his or her final breaths. It may be at the funeral of a friend. It may even be at a moment when we would expect uncompromised joy, such as the birth of a child.

Celtic spirituality, which arose in Ireland and the British Isles between A.D. 300 and 600, included a concept of "thinness." The Celts would say, "It was a thin time" or "It was a thin place." What they meant was that the "thick wall" between humanity and eternity, between the physical and spiritual world, had become more permeable. There are many times and places when it's easy not to think about God at all. But there are other times and places where you almost feel his presence. There's a sense of vastness, a feeling that much more is out there than you've ever realized before. It may be in the middle of the night, when you awaken and feel that the circumstances of this material world seem especially "thin" and you wonder what lies ahead.

Sometimes you get ambushed in the strangest moments. That's what happened to a man who approached me feeling very troubled after the birth of his little girl. It didn't make sense, because the girl was healthy and everything was going great. But I've learned over the years to be quiet and listen to what is on a person's heart.

He said, "Doug, I have to tell you something, but you're going to think I'm crazy."

I replied, "Brother, I love you no matter what. Nothing you can tell me would make me love you less."

"Well, the first time I held my daughter and looked into her face, I felt really, really sad. I haven't even told my wife this."

"Why were you so sad?"

"Because I know someday she is going to die. Am I crazy?"

He was experiencing a "thin moment." He realized, as many of us eventually do, that the beginning and ending of life can be very close.

What do you believe? Have you experienced any "thin moments," any brief glimpses into eternity? Or, as a child of this skeptical age, do you find it hard to believe in heaven?

IT'S HARD TO BELIEVE IN HEAVEN BECAUSE WE LIVE IN A RELATIVELY COMFORTABLE AGE

It's hard to believe in heaven when earth is so comfortable and death seems so far away. As one man said, only half-jokingly, "Why do I need heaven when I've got my swimming pool and hot tub?"

While it's true that there is tremendous pain and suffering in the world, it's also true that our generation has more medical care, more financial prosperity, and more creature comforts than any people living at any other time in history. During the Middle Ages, most children died before the age of five. Families were very blessed if they saw more than one child make it to adulthood. The average adult life span was about half of what it is today. Death was often a daily reality. By comparison, life isn't all that bad right now. Despite the reality of suffering, this is a fairly good time to be alive.

Is it hard for you to believe in heaven because your life is so comfortable now?

IT'S HARD TO BELIEVE IN HEAVEN BECAUSE WE LIVE IN AN ACTIVITY-ADDICTED AGE

Many of us are too busy to think about heaven. The pace of life, along with the volume and nature of our everyday activities, lures us from heavenly pursuits. Most of us are doing, doing, doing—filling every moment with work, learning, technology, entertainment, recreation, and relationships. We are caught in this whirling, worldly tornado called living. Since heaven is intangible and invisible, it never even enters into our consciousness. And if it does, we usually consider it only briefly because we have no frame of reference for it. Then comes an interruption—the sudden death of a loved one or a famous celebrity—and all the activity seems pointless.

BUT THEN AGAIN, IT'S HARD NOT TO BELIEVE IN HEAVEN

As a kindergartner, my favorite books were about dinosaurs, whose toenails I imagined as being bigger than my whole house—who could eat the local grocery store for an appetizer. I shuddered at the fierce pterodactyl, that batlike reptile. And the Tyrannosaurus rex—well, words fail to describe the terror I imagined: being caught in the viselike grip of those claws, being thrust toward his reeking mouth. . . . Oh my!

Now that I've taken a step back from the vivid imagination of childhood, I've tried to understand why so many of us are fascinated with dinosaurs. I think the reason might be this: *We are fascinated by a reality we've never experienced—something we can hardly imagine, but for which there is credible evidence of existence.* We are people of the five senses, but we find our greatest fascination in a sixth sense: the imagination. And imagination is one of the primary organs of faith. Heaven, life eternal, is planted within our heart (see Ecclesiastes 3:11), but we can hardly imagine such a strange, different, and wonderful mode of existence. But while thoughts of dinosaurs may be an interesting form of entertainment, thoughts of heaven can serve very practical purposes. Puritan preacher Richard Baxter wrote that thinking of heaven as our eternal rest "is not our comfort only, but our stability. Our liveliness in all duties, our enduring of tribulation, our honoring of God, the vigor of our love, thankfulness, and all our graces, yea, the very being of our religion and Christianity, depend on the believing, serious thoughts of our rest [in heaven]."[3]

Jesus said to his disciples, "I am going there to prepare a place for you. And if I go and prepare a place for you, I will come back and take you to be with me that you also may be where I am" (John 14:2-3).

Think of that place. Let your imagination feast on thoughts of dwelling in God's house. Ponder the beauty;

the joy; the freedom of heart, mind, body, and soul. Our destination is not extinction but eternity. God's best is yet to be!

WHERE DO WE GO FROM HERE?

As far as I can tell, there are four options for what we might believe about life after death:

- When we die, we cease to exist.
- When we die, we all go to heaven.
- When we die, we keep coming back.
- When we die, we are judged, with one of two possible destinations.

WHEN WE DIE, WE CEASE TO EXIST

This view is called *annihilationism*. Annihilationism says that when we die, that's it. It's all over. We're done. Any immortality comes from the legacy we leave in our children, from memories our friends (who will soon die) have of us, or from our reputation.

Annihilationism is one of the harshest doctrines I've ever heard. The apostle Paul said, "If only for this life we have hope in Christ, we are to be pitied more than all men" (1 Corinthians 15:19). It's as if Paul is saying, "If we only believe in Jesus for this life, we're pitiful."

Even many people who find it hard to believe in God find it hard to believe in annihilationism. They experience the longing that won't let go. As the writer of Ecclesiastes said, "He has made everything beautiful in its time. He has also set eternity in the hearts of men"

(Ecclesiastes 3:11). People long for more beyond these earthly days. You can see it in the megalithic tombs that were built thousands of years before Christ. They were based on a belief in an afterlife. Throughout history, people have believed in life after death. That's what the ancient Egyptian pyramids are all about. The testimony of the human heart is that this world isn't all there is.

WHEN WE DIE, WE ALL GO TO HEAVEN

Many people simply believe that we will all go to heaven, regardless of our belief—or lack of belief—in God; regardless of our obedience—or lack of obedience—to God's commands. This view, called *universalism,* became widespread in New England in the 1880s and has continued as a strong trend in modern theology.

While universalism has the appeal of appearing "tolerant," it contradicts Scripture and our sense of what is just. God's Word reveals that God desires the salvation of all people (see 1 Timothy 2:4) and gave his Son for the salvation of the world (John 3:16). But we must accept God's love in faith and manifest that faith through obedience. We will see more clearly in the coming chapters that universalism makes a mockery of all that God has done in Christ.

WHEN WE DIE, WE KEEP COMING BACK

Many people, especially those who practice Eastern religions, believe in some form of reincarnation. The mystical religions of the Orient, especially Hinduism and Buddhism, teach the concept of *Karma. Karma* is a Sanskrit word for "work" or "action." According to the concept of Karma, every action has inevitable consequences. These consequences attach themselves to the doer, requiring reward or punishment. Reward and punishment are carried out through a cycle of rebirth, during which people must work out, in successive reincarnations, the damnable consequences of their sin and folly. Following this logic, the inequalities and struggles of life are the consequences of actions (Karma) in previous lives. Likewise, our works, thoughts, and deeds in this life inexorably fix our lot in future existence. When we die, our Karma is judged, and our soul comes back into a new body or form of being. Whether we come back as a worm or a priest depends on how we behaved in this life. Those who were good will move up the scale of beings; those who were bad will go down the scale of beings. This cycle of rebirth is supposed to purge sin and satisfy cosmic justice.

Belief in reincarnation denies everything Jesus Christ did on the cross. It flies in the face of the doctrine of salvation by grace alone through Christ alone. As Donald Bloesch writes, "In evangelical Christianity . . . the burden of sin or Karma is borne by Christ himself. He frees us from the curse of the law, from the deleterious effects of our sin."[4]

WHEN WE DIE, WE ARE JUDGED

The Bible teaches another view about what happens when we die: We will be judged. The author of Hebrews writes, "And just as it is destined that each person dies only once and after that comes judgment" (Hebrews 9:27, NLT). There will come a time when all accounts will be settled. Evil will be punished, and good will be rewarded. Jesus spoke about the judgment and consequences that await us immediately following this life. His teaching in the Sermon on the Mount is a clear example:

> If your right eye causes you to sin, gouge it out and throw it away. It is better for you to lose one part of your body than for your whole body to be thrown into hell. And if your right hand causes you to sin, cut it off and throw it away. It is better for you to lose one part of your body than for your whole body to go into hell. (Matthew 5:29-30)

There is no reference to Karma, to returning again, or to everybody's being saved. The clear message is that we will be called to answer for our actions.

We'll discuss the specific nature of judgment in chapter 3. For now it is enough to realize that there are four basic possibilities concerning our destiny after death. What's more, believing in heaven and hell is not escaping reality. It is facing the reality outlined in the Bible.

WHAT IF THERE REALLY IS A HEAVEN—AND A HELL?

Let's say there really is a heaven and a hell. Let's say that there really is a time when each of us will stand before God and answer for what we have done in this life. That we will give an account of how we've kept—and not kept—God's commandments. That we will answer for what we've done with the resources and gifts he's entrusted to us. Let's suppose that's what will really happen. What difference would that make?

EVERYTHING WE DO WILL ONE DAY BE KNOWN

Just think of the difference it would make if you knew your every thought and action were being filmed on video or recorded on tape to broadcast on the six o'clock news! The Bible says, "For there is nothing hidden that will not be disclosed, and nothing concealed that will not be known or brought out into the open" (Luke 8:17). Some of our actions will be made known in this lifetime, in public. Other things, however, will only be revealed before the judgment seat of God. Does that knowledge affect the way you live? Does it affect the decisions you make, your priorities, and your perspective on life?

WE CAN BREAK FREE FROM PEER PRESSURE

When you live for heaven, you can find a wonderful freedom from the pressures and attractions of this world. Instead of living for an audience of critics, you can live to hear the Lord say, "Well done, good and faithful servant." Even Cicero, the Roman writer, statesman, and orator, found courage because of a belief in immortality. He said, "It is only the instinct of immortality which makes us spend our lives in toils and dangers."[5]

WE HAVE FEWER THINGS TO WORRY ABOUT

Living in the light of eternity tells you not only what you have to take seriously but also what you don't have to worry about. What others think of you doesn't really matter. What matters is what God thinks of you. Ultimately you've got to answer to God and God alone.

DOES IT MATTER?

Does it matter what you believe about heaven and hell? Yes, it does, because your desired destination determines your plans. Understanding what lies ahead shapes the way you live and the way you die.

I once heard T. S. Eliot quoted as saying that in a world of fugitives, anyone who takes a different direction appears to be running away. If you choose to believe in heaven and hell, it may look like you're running away. But, in fact, deciding to consider the reality of heaven and hell may be the most courageous—the wisest—decision you'll ever make.

So what do you believe about life after death? What does the Bible say about it? How can you be sure you're going to go to heaven? Is hell a real place with flames and demons? Or is it just a metaphor or scare tactic?

Those are the kinds of questions we're going to explore in the coming chapters.

NOTES

1. J. I. Packer, *God's Words* (Downers Grove, Ill.: InterVarsity Press, 1981), 202.

2. Douglas J. Rumford, *Scared to Life* (Wheaton, Ill.: Victor Books, 1994), 104. Adapted from *Our Daily Bread,* 1994 Radio Bible Class, Grand Rapids, April 2, 1994.

3. Richard Baxter, *The Saints' Everlasting Rest* (Grand Rapids: Baker Book House, 1978), 17.

4. Compiled from Donald Bloesch, *Essentials of Evangelical Theology* (San Francisco: Harper & Row, 1978), 170, and *Eerdman's Handbook to the World's Religions* (Grand Rapids: Eerdmans Publishing Co., 1982), 189–90, 411, 426.

5. Quoted in E. E. Holmes, *Immortality,* in *The Oxford Library of Practical Theology* (London: Longmans, Green, and Co., 1908), 11.

CHAPTER TWO

"What Is Heaven Like?"

Imagine the following conversation between a worm and a caterpillar:

> "So are you gettin' ready?" asks the worm.
> "For what?" replies the caterpillar.
> "You know!"
> "What?"
> "*Sheesh!* Yeah, right, like you don't know!"
> "I don't know what you're talking about!" insists the caterpillar.
> "You're gonna leave, forget about me, and go soaring off on those great big wings! You're gonna change!"
> "Leave? Change? Why? I like it here! What am I gonna change into?"
> "You mean you really don't know?"
> "Know what? Look, you've been watching too much of *The X-Files* or something! I don't like you pulling my legs!"

"You're in what they call the larva stage."

"Don't you talk like that!"

"Look, it's a fact of life. You're going into a chrysalis, and your body will change."

"But I like my body! It can do all these curving things. And my legs . . . have you ever seen such synchronization of movement in your life? Man, it's beautiful. I can walk straight up a stem, hang upside down . . . what could be better?"

"Flying," says the worm.

"Flying!" exclaims the caterpillar. "But I'm scared of heights!"

"I have a feeling you'll forget about all that. Especially when you're sipping nectar from the flowers."

"But I hate flowers! I just like these leaves."

"Man, if you knew what's coming . . ."

"Hmmm, that's weird. . . ."

"What is?" asks the worm.

"I just feel like curling up and going to sleep. I think I'll start making that blanket. Now . . . don't you go anywhere . . . ," says the caterpillar with a yawn, his voice trailing off in sleep.

"Oh, don't fret. I won't leave. But you will . . . and are you ever gonna be amazed!"

The worm gets it, but the caterpillar just can't imagine what he's in for. I would like to ask you: What do you think you're in for? Do you have a sense that you will undergo a *major* change in the next life? Even as the caterpillar cannot fathom the radical transformation that awaits him, neither can any of us! Life with God in heaven is the believer's highest hope. It is our greatest comfort. It is a primary motivation in life for faith and obedience. But most of us really don't get it. We can't imagine a heavenly life any more than the caterpillar in the story could.

WE'VE BEEN CREATED FOR SO MUCH MORE

God did not create humanity for a limited existence. He created us for eternal fellowship with himself. We have lost this sense of a heavenly destiny—and the loss has stunted our human experience, lowered our expectations, and greatly limited our perspective. It's time to recapture a vision of our destiny. In the previous chapter, we considered the fact that our desired destination should determine our planning and should shape every aspect of our life. Now we will begin to look at the nature of heaven.

We are not given much detail about heaven in the Bible. But by the glimpses we are given we know that we are going to be amazed. As Paul says in 1 Corinthians 2:9: "No eye has seen, no ear has heard, no mind has conceived what God has prepared for those who love him."

Heaven is beyond our wildest imaginations and expectations, but there are still a few things that have been revealed. In this chapter we will consider three characteristics of heaven. In heaven:

- God completes our transformation.
- God fulfills our deepest longings.
- God welcomes us into eternal, joyful fellowship with himself.

IN HEAVEN, GOD COMPLETES OUR TRANSFORMATION

Revelation 21:1-7 presents us with an intriguing glimpse of heaven.

> Then I saw a new heaven and a new earth, for the old heaven and the old earth had disappeared. And the sea was also gone. And I saw the holy city, the new Jerusalem, coming down from God out of heaven like a beautiful bride prepared for her husband.
>
> I heard a loud shout from the throne, saying, "Look, the home of God is now among his people! He will live with them, and they will be his people. God himself will be with them. He will remove all of their sorrows, and there will be no more death or sorrow or crying or pain. For the old world and its evils are gone forever."
>
> And the one sitting on the throne said, "Look, I am making all things new!" And then he said to me, "Write this down, for what I tell you is trustworthy and true." And he also said, "It is finished! I am the Alpha and the Omega—the Beginning and the End. To all who are thirsty I will give the springs of the water of life without charge! All who are victorious will inherit all

these blessings, and I will be their God, and they
will be my children. (NLT)

GOD WILL MAKE ALL THINGS NEW

Note especially the verse that says, "And the one sitting
on the throne said, 'Look, I am making all things new!'"
There are two words used for "new" in the Greek. The
first is *neos*. *Neos* refers to chronological or temporal
newness, like newly blossoming flowers or new clothes.
The second word, *kainos*, means *qualitatively* new, like
something we've never seen before—something previously unknown, unprecedented, marvelous!

Several summers ago our family visited the Smithso-
nian Institution. (I might note that we went through the
exhibits very quickly with younger children!) One thing
that fascinated me was studying the history of computer
development. We saw pictures of the first computer
with its vacuum tubes filling huge rooms. This early
computer could do little more than perform the functions we now carry out on a handheld calculator. Why?
Because the microchip hadn't been invented yet. The
microchip is *kainos*. It is totally, radically new. Look at a
room full of vacuum tubes, and then hold up a microchip. This is something we never could have imagined!

Technology has given us numerous examples of
kainos. Consider the difference between a phonograph
and a compact disc: The digital compact disc that is
read by light was *kainos* to people who used phono-
graphs played by a mechanical needle. Compare a two-
dimensional picture and a hologram: A hologram
is qualitatively new. It gives you a sense that you're

looking at a three-dimensional object projected into space. It's unprecedented, something you could not have imagined before.

When we talk about heaven, we're talking about *kainos,* a level of existence that is qualitatively different from anything we've ever experienced or could even imagine. In this life on earth, you and I are like vacuum tubes!

WE WILL RECEIVE A RESURRECTION BODY

What will our resurrection body be like? Theologians have speculated a great deal on this subject. The Roman Catholic theologian Thomas Aquinas (1225–74) came up with an idea based on Ephesians 4:13, which says that we are to grow up into the stature of the fullness of Jesus Christ. Aquinas deduced that Jesus was thirty years old in the stature of the fullness of his physical humanity. Therefore, asserted Aquinas, our resurrection body will probably be like the one we had when we were thirty years old. (That may or may not encourage you.) My personal sense is that we shouldn't try to speculate too much. The Bible does give us some hints, however, to encourage us.

Paul contrasts the difference between our mortal and resurrection bodies by using the analogy of a seed. He writes in 1 Corinthians 15:35-44:

> But someone may ask, "How will the dead be raised? What kind of bodies will they have?" What a foolish question! When you put a seed into the ground, it doesn't grow into a plant

unless it dies first. And what you put in the ground is not the plant that will grow, but only a dry little seed of wheat or whatever it is you are planting. Then God gives it a new body—just the kind he wants it to have. A different kind of plant grows from each kind of seed. And just as there are different kinds of seeds and plants, so also there are different kinds of flesh—whether of humans, animals, birds, or fish.

There are bodies in the heavens, and there are bodies on earth. The glory of the heavenly bodies is different from the beauty of the earthly bodies. The sun has one kind of glory, while the moon and stars each have another kind. And even the stars differ from each other in their beauty and brightness.

It is the same way for the resurrection of the dead. Our earthly bodies, which die and decay, will be different when they are resurrected, for they will never die. Our bodies now disappoint us, but when they are raised, they will be full of glory. They are weak now, but when they are raised, they will be full of power. They are natural human bodies now, but when they are raised, they will be spiritual bodies. For just as there are natural bodies, so also there are spiritual bodies. (NLT)

A seed falls into the ground and dies, and then it grows into something totally different. Could you tell, especially if you're not an expert, what kind of plant you're going to get from a particular little seed? Will it become a giant redwood or a fragrant rose or a majestic oak? Just looking at the tiny seed, it's hard to imagine. So it is with the resurrection body—we cannot fully imagine it. Scripture, however, reveals several principles about the nature of our bodily existence in heaven.

WE WILL CONTINUE AS UNIQUE INDIVIDUALS AND BE ABLE TO RECOGNIZE ONE ANOTHER IN HEAVEN

When Jesus took Peter, James, and John to the Mount of Transfiguration, they recognized the heavenly visitors they saw there as Moses and Elijah, who had died long before (see Mark 9:4). And when Jesus spoke of God as being the God of Abraham, Isaac, and Jacob, he spoke of them as presently existing, not simply as people from the past: "But now, as to whether there will be a resurrection of the dead—haven't you ever read about this in the Scriptures? Long after Abraham, Isaac, and Jacob had died, God said, 'I am the God of Abraham, the God of Isaac, and the God of Jacob.' So he is the God of the living, not the dead" (Matthew 22:31-32, NLT). Jesus again spoke of Abraham, Isaac, and Jacob's continued existence as unique individuals when he talked about the great banquet at the culmination of history: "And I tell you this, that many Gentiles will come from all over the world and sit down with Abraham, Isaac, and Jacob at the feast in the Kingdom of Heaven" (Matthew 8:11, NLT).

Some have wondered whether our resurrection body will be recognizable, since the two disciples on the road to Emmaus didn't immediately recognize the man walking with them as the resurrected Jesus. The disciples' "blindness" may have been due to a number of factors. They may have been preoccupied with their own grief. Or perhaps Jesus deliberately kept his features hidden. We aren't told the reasons for the disciples' delayed recognition. Eventually, however, when Jesus broke bread with them, perhaps revealing the nail prints in his hands, the disciples knew him.

The concept that our resurrection body will be recognizable is consistent with God's valuing each of us as unique individuals who will continue as his children through all eternity. We will not be absorbed into some impersonal force or cut off from our unique history and personality.

OUR RESURRECTION BODY WILL BE
A SPIRITUAL BODY

Having a spiritual body doesn't mean that you're going to look like Casper the friendly ghost! Your spiritual body won't necessarily be immaterial, without substance, a form that others can see right through. *Spiritual* means "subject to the power of the Holy Spirit." If you said, "So-and-so is a really spiritual person," it doesn't mean you can put your hand through that person as he or she walks by. It means the person's life is guided by spiritual things, by the Lord.

In heaven we will wholly cooperate with the Holy Spirit. We will no longer fight temptations. We will no longer struggle to do good. We will want to do good. We will have no inclination toward evil. In fact, evil won't be a possibility.

OUR RESURRECTION BODY WILL BE
A GLORIOUS BODY

We will have a body that shares in the glory of Jesus
Christ. In 1 John 3:1-3 we read:

> See how very much our heavenly Father loves us,
> for he allows us to be called his children, and
> we really are! But the people who belong to this
> world don't know God, so they don't understand
> that we are his children. Yes, dear friends, we
> are already God's children, and we can't even
> imagine what we will be like when Christ returns.
> But we do know that when he comes we will be
> like him, for we will see him as he really is. And
> all who believe this will keep themselves pure,
> just as Christ is pure. (NLT)

We will be like Jesus, sharing in his glory. Our glory,
of course, will not be equal to his. He is the unique
Son of God. But somehow, we will share in Christ's
glory, as children share in the blessings of a parent's
success or as citizens share in the peace and prosperity
of a nation.

C. S. Lewis, in his sermon, "The Weight of Glory,"
gives us an intriguing glimpse into the glory that awaits
us in Christ:

> It may be possible for each to think too much
> of his own potential glory hereafter; it is hardly
> possible for him to think too often or too
> deeply about that of his neighbor. The load,

or weight, or burden of my neighbor's glory should be laid daily on my back, a load so heavy that only humility can carry it, and that backs of the proud will be broken. It is a serious thing to live in a society of possible gods and goddesses, to remember that the dullest and most uninteresting person you talk to may one day be a creature which, if you saw it now, you would be strongly tempted to worship, or else a horror and a corruption such as you now met, if at all, only in a nightmare. . . .

There are no ordinary people. You have never talked to a mere mortal. Nations, cultures, arts, civilization—these are mortal, and their life is to ours as the life of a gnat. But it is immortals whom we joke with, work with, marry, snub, and exploit—immortal horrors or everlasting splendors. This does not mean that we are to be perpetually solemn. We must play. But our merriment must be of that kind (and it is, in fact, the merriest kind) which exists between people who have, from the outset, taken each other seriously—no flippancy, no superiority, no presumption. And our charity must be a real and costly love, with deep feeling for the sins in spite of which we love the sinner—no mere tolerance or indulgence which parodies love as flippancy parodies merriment.

Next to the Blessed Sacrament itself, your neighbor is the holiest object presented to your senses. If he is your Christian neighbor he is holy

in almost the same way, for in him also Christ
vere latitat—the glorifier and the glorified, Glory
himself, is truly hidden.[1]

OUR RESURRECTION BODY WILL BE IMMORTAL

When we have our resurrection body, we will be inde-
structible. We'll be forever vital and energetic. Incorruptible. Strong. Resilient. We'll be impervious to any
attack or any problem. There will be no aging in
heaven. No degeneration. No decay.

As a teenager, Joni Eareckson-Tada dove off a dock
into the Chesapeake Bay, hit a rock, and snapped her
neck. The accident left her a quadriplegic. Joni says that
while she wrestles with her present condition, she is
grateful for God's care—and has hope for the future.

> OK, I am paralyzed. It's terrible, I don't like
> it. But can God still use me, paralyzed? Can I,
> paralyzed, still worship God and love Him? He
> has taught me that I can. Maybe God's gift to me
> is my dependence on him. I will never reach the
> place where I'm self-sufficient, where God is
> crowded out of my life. I'm aware of his grace
> to me every moment.
>
> My need for help is obvious every day when
> I wake up, flat on my back, waiting for someone
> to come dress me. I can't even comb my hair or
> blow my nose alone! But I have friends who care.
> I have the beauty of the scenery. With my art
> sales, I can even support myself financially—the
> dream of a handicapped person. The peace that

counts is an internal peace, and God has lavished me with that peace.

And there's one more thing. I have hope for the future. The Bible speaks of our body being "glorified" in heaven. In high school that was always a hazy, foreign concept. But now I realize that I will be healed. I haven't been cheated out of being a complete person—I'm just going through a forty-year delay, and God is with me even through that. Being "glorified"—I know the meaning of that now. It's the time, after my death here, when I'll be on my feet dancing.[2]

God is going to do a new—qualitatively new—thing in heaven. He will complete our transformation. Joni's image of transformation is dancing. What is yours?

This much we know about transformation: We will no longer battle with sin and its consequences in this fallen world. We will not experience injuries, tragedies, and injustice. Instead, God's care will keep us whole. Our transformed body will be fit for a life in eternal glory.

IN HEAVEN, GOD FULFILLS OUR DEEPEST LONGINGS

Even at its best, this life always leaves us a bit dissatisfied. Our experiences never quite live up to our expectations. Our dreams often go unfulfilled. Disappointment can overwhelm us. We long for so much more. The fact is, our longings are signs of eternity in our heart. C. S. Lewis said, "If I find in myself a desire which no experience in this world can satisfy, the most probable explanation is that I was made for another world."[3]

The day will come when our disappointments will vanish and we will receive our heart's desires. That day is described in Revelation 21:4. "He will remove all of their sorrows, and there will be no more death or sorrow or crying or pain. For the old world and its evils are gone forever" (Revelation 24:4, NLT). The Revised Standard Version says the Lord "will wipe away every tear from their eyes." I don't know if there's a more intimate picture in the Bible of what heaven will be like. Think about the things that make you cry, that make you mourn. God will dry your tears. He will fulfill your deepest longings. Can you imagine that?

HEAVEN MEANS NO MORE SPOILED PLEASURES

Heaven means the bliss of full fellowship with the triune God—the ultimate fulfillment of life. It means a new (kainos) heaven and a new (kainos) earth without the consequences of the Fall, of decay, of sin, of pollution, of mortality, of human frailness, of human vulnerability. Those things will be gone.

Words fail to capture this reality. Perhaps it is best portrayed in images from daily life.

Heaven is like being out in the sun as long as you want without getting a sunburn.
Heaven is like enjoying playing ball in your yard without any worry about breaking windows or damaging the plants.

Heaven is like a picnic without ants.

Heaven is like sitting outside on a summer evening with no mosquitoes or flies.

Heaven is like eating any food you want with no worries about calories or cholesterol.

Heaven is like planting a crop and having no weeds.

Heaven is like walking through a park at night, enjoying the cool breezes, with no fear at all.

How do you imagine heaven? Think about your own "spoiled pleasures." Think about what it would be like if your pleasures were unspoiled. Does this help you picture what heaven will be like?

HEAVEN MEANS THE FULFILLMENT OF OUR CAPACITIES

In addition to removing the negatives that have ruined our life, heaven will bring the fulfillment of the positive capacities that are inherent in the creation. A. A. Hodge, a Presbyterian professor of theology at Princeton Seminary in the 1880s, described life in heaven as fulfilling the potential we sense is possible but unreachable on earth.

The eternal home of the Divine Human Being will have all the necessary and thoroughly human structures, conditions, and activities. Its joys and activities must all be rational, moral, emotional, voluntary, and active. There must be the exercise of all the facilities. The gratification of all the tastes; the development of all talent capacities;

the realization of all ideas; the reason; the
intellectual curiosity; the imagination; our
aesthetic instincts; our holy affections; our
social affinities. The inexhaustible resources of
strength and power native to the human soul
must all find in Heaven exercise and satisfaction.
There must always be a goal of endeavor before
us ever future.[4]

Professor Hodge is saying that what gives us the most
meaning in our life here on earth will be fulfilled in
heaven. We will continue to develop our gifts. The
things we love to do on earth—because of God-given
desires that I call "echoes of heaven"—will be transformed by being fulfilled.

My personal theory is that heaven is a place where we
will develop all the talents and abilities that we possess
as human beings. I believe that through all eternity we
will enjoy the fullest expression of our humanity as beings created in God's image. I sometimes like to think
that I'll be able to take organ lessons from J. S. Bach,
learn to paint like Leonardo da Vinci, and discuss
writing with C. S. Lewis and J. R. R. Tolkien. Maybe
I'll even make up my own stories like Lewis's Chroni-
cles of Narnia or Tolkien's The Hobbit or Lord of the
Rings.

You likely have very different interests than I do,
but I believe heaven will be the fulfillment of your desires. The heaven I envision is very different from the
stereotypes. Mark Twain is quoted as having said,
"Well, as I understand it, in heaven all you do is float

around on the clouds and play a harp all day. But if that isn't hell, I don't know what is!"

I think Twain missed the point. We will be gathered around the throne of the Lord in worship and glory and praise of his name, but we also will have all eternity to spend in joyful activity. Life in heaven will include the fullest expression of who we are as human beings.

Ultimately, however, heaven is not about what happens to us or even about what we get to do. The ultimate truth of heaven is that God welcomes us into the eternal, joyful fellowship of love and worship that he prepared for us from the foundation of the earth.

IN HEAVEN GOD WELCOMES US INTO ETERNAL, JOYFUL FELLOWSHIP OF LOVE AND WORSHIP

Remember what Dorothy said in *The Wizard of Oz*? "There's no place like home." Let me tell you this: There's no home like heaven.

Coming home from college, I was so glad to be out of the dormitory that I'd walk through our house saying, "Hello, kitchen! Hello, family room! Hello, TV!" Then I'd go back into my bedroom and say, "Hello, bed," especially after that horrible college bunk I had. There was no home like my own. There's no place like home, but there's no home like heaven!

Heaven is more than cosmic geography. The essence of heaven is relationship: being at home with our heavenly Father. Revelation 21:3 says, "Look, the home of God is now among his people! He will live with them, and they will be his people. God himself will be with them" (NLT). When the Bible says that God will live with us, it means that we will be at home in his family. Paul says in Romans 8:17 that we will be co-heirs with Jesus Christ. Because of our relationship with him, we will receive an inheritance that is, in some way, equal to Christ's! This truly boggles the mind.

Meister Eckehart, a Christian mystic of the thirteenth century, said, "God gives us the greatest gift of all, the gift of Himself."[5] Heaven is God's home, a home he shares with his loyal heavenly hosts and his redeemed people. Being in heaven will be like being at a family reunion. It will include a full reconciliation with people "from every nation and tribe and people and language" (Revelation 7:9, NLT). All God's children will finally be one, and all the hurts and barriers will disappear. We will experience joyful, restful, healing, renewing fellowship. We will see God's face.

No sermon or book can fully capture what lies in store for those who love the Lord. It's been said, "Unless it were too vast for our intellectual comprehension, it would be too narrow for our spiritual needs."[6] I can't begin to imagine what heaven will be like, but this much I know: We're going to be amazed.

At the conclusion of *The Last Battle*, the final book in the Narnia series, C. S. Lewis describes the experiences of Lucy, Peter, and Edmond, who, suddenly finding themselves back in the land of Narnia, are greatly confused. In the chapter titled "Farewell to Shadowlands," Lewis writes:

Lucy said, "We're so afraid of being sent away, Aslan. [Aslan is the lion, the Christ-figure in the story.] And you have sent us back into our own world so often."

"No fear of that," said Aslan. "Have you not guessed?"

Their hearts leaped in a wild hope within them.

"There *was* a real railway accident," said Aslan softly. "Your father and your mother and all of you are—as you used to call it in the Shadowlands— dead. The term is over: the holidays have begun. The dream has ended: this is the morning!"

And as He spoke He no longer looked to them like a lion; but the things that began to happen after that were so great and beautiful that I cannot write them. And for us this is the end of all the stories, and we can most truly say that they all lived happily ever after. But for them it was only the beginning of the real story. All their life in this world and all their adventures in Narnia had only been the cover and the title page: now at last they were beginning Chapter One of the Great Story which no one on earth has read: which goes on forever: in which every chapter is better than the one before.[7]

Do you know what awaits you on the other side of death? Think back to our caterpillar friend. He just didn't get it. But that didn't keep him from changing. And even though we don't fully understand what lies ahead, that doesn't mean we won't change. In heaven, the Lord will complete our transformation. He will fulfill our deepest longings. He will welcome us into eternal, joyful fellowship of love and worship.

We're going to be amazed. May that hope, that desired destination, affect every plan of this day.

NOTES

1. C. S. Lewis, *The Weight of Glory* (Grand Rapids: William B. Eerdmans Publishing Company, 1949), 14–15.

2. Philip Yancey, *Where Is God When It Hurts?* (Grand Rapids: Zondervan Publishing House, 1977), 118–120.

3. C. S. Lewis, *Mere Christianity* (New York: Macmillan Publishing Co., Inc., 1952), 120.

4. Peter Toon, *Heaven and Hell: A Biblical and Theological Overview* (Nashville: Thomas Nelson Publishers, 1986), 157–58, citing A. A. Hodge, *Evangelical Theology* (Edinburgh, 1976), 399–402.

5. Quoted in Elizabeth O'Connor, *Eighth Day of Creation* (Waco: Word Books, 1971), 110–111.

6. Balfour, *Foundations of Belief* (p. 259), in E. E. Holmes, *Immortality,* in *The Oxford Library of Practical Theology* (London: Longmans, Green, and Co., 1908), 11.

7. C. S. Lewis, *The Last Battle* (New York: Scholastic., Inc., 1956), 210–11.

CHAPTER THREE

"What Will Judgment Day Be Like?"

My son and I were walking toward a beautiful white chapel on a stone pathway that wound its way through a burial ground with weathered grave markers and centuries-old monuments. I was to be the guest preacher at this New England church dating from the early 1700s. "Why did they build the graveyard so you have to walk through it on the way to church?" my son asked me. "Was it to scare people?"

The custom of building a burial ground around a church dates back centuries to congregations in Europe. Contrary to my son's suspicions, the practice wasn't developed to frighten people into faith. Rather, it arose from the desire to be buried in consecrated or holy ground. But it also served as a vivid reminder of the ultimate fact of death, a fact most of us want to avoid.

Many of us are uncomfortable speaking directly about death. Instead of saying, "Bill died," we may say something like, "he passed away."

However we refer to it, death is a reality we cannot

avoid. More sobering still is the fact that not only will we die, but we will also be judged. Hebrews 9:27 says, "It is appointed unto men once to die, but after this the judgment" (KJV).

Any study of heaven requires us to consider the criteria for entering it. Will everyone go to heaven no matter what? Or is heaven perhaps reserved for a few especially good people? Is there something we must do to be sure we will go to heaven? These are questions we will consider in this chapter.

WHAT ABOUT JUDGMENT DAY?

On the south porch of Chartres Cathedral in France is one of the most powerful depictions of the Last Judgment in all sacred art and sculpture. Above the cathedral's central bay of doors Christ is seated, showing his earthly wounds. On either side of Christ are Mary, his mother, and John. Above Christ to his extreme left and right are angels, holding the instruments of his crucifixion: the scourge (whip), the post to which he was tied for flogging, the spear that pierced his side, and the cross. Other angels are blowing the trumpets that herald Judgment Day, and the heavenly court is assembled to judge all humanity. Around the seated Christ are scores of the dead, coming up from their graves to face their sentencing. The damned, their fingers turned downward, are hurled by demons into hell. The redeemed, their fingers turned upward, are entering the New Jerusalem. One of the most tender scenes shows Abraham with three small childlike figures, portraying the blessed who will be rocked in the bosom of Abraham (see Luke 16:19-31). Words fail to capture the power of this scene of final decision, when every human being will confront his or her ultimate destiny.

The idea that a person might go to hell isn't a popular concept in our day, but it is the clear teaching of God's Word. The book of Revelation gives us a vivid presentation of Judgment Day:

> And I saw a great white throne, and I saw the one who was sitting on it. The earth and sky fled from his presence, but they found no place to hide. I saw the dead, both great and small, standing before God's throne. And the books were opened, including the Book of Life. And the dead were judged according to the things written in the books, according to what they had done. The sea gave up the dead in it, and death and the grave gave up the dead in them. They were all judged according to their deeds. And death and the grave were thrown into the lake of fire. This is the second death—the lake of fire. And anyone whose name was not found recorded in the Book of Life was thrown into the lake of fire. (Revelation 20:11-15, NLT)

EVERY PERSON WILL BE JUDGED

Countless books have been written about the near-death experiences of people who do not profess faith in Christ but who claim to have seen heaven. Some speak of passing through a tunnel and approaching a great white light. Some tell of experiencing a feeling of great peace and love. But I have personally heard several accounts that are not nearly so pleasant. For example, one man told me this about his near-death experience: "I saw demons and angels fighting over my soul and body. I could see both the beauty of heaven and the horror of hell. I cried out for mercy. It was absolutely terrifying. I had never believed in Jesus up to that time, but I promised God that if I lived, I would trust him. When I prayed that, I could feel the demons letting go."

I cannot explain the nature and meaning of near-death experiences. In any case, I don't want to gamble my eternal welfare on the basis of other people's reported experiences. The only reliable guide to the future is the Bible, which tells us that Jesus consistently taught the reality of judgment. For example, in the parable of the Talents, Jesus speaks of the faithful being rewarded and the wicked being cast into outer darkness where there will be weeping and gnashing of teeth (see Matthew 25:29-30). In fact, eight major parables of Jesus teach about judgment: the Ten Virgins (Matthew 25:1-13), the Wise and Faithful Servants (Matthew 24:45-51; Luke 12:42-48), the Traveling Boss (Mark 13:34-37), the Two Sons (Matthew 21:28-32), the Wicked Farmers (Matthew 21:33-46; Mark 12:1-9; Luke 20:9-16), the Unproductive Fig Tree (Luke 13:6-9), the Marriage Feast (Matthew 22:1-14), and the Unforgiving Servant (Matthew 18:23-35).[1]

Judgment is so serious a matter that God has delayed

the return of Christ in order to give people the opportunity to repent. "The Lord is not slow in keeping his promise, as some understand slowness. He is patient with you, not wanting anyone to perish, but everyone to come to repentance" (2 Peter 3:9).

According to the Bible, there are actually two judgments. All of us will be judged at least once, and some of us will be judged twice. The first judgment, which is for everyone, is the judgment of life and of death.

THE FIRST JUDGMENT: LIFE OR DEATH

When you and I die, we will appear before the Lord, who will look to see if our name is written in the Book of Life.

You could think of the Book of Life as the official roll book of the citizens of heaven. How does your name get written in the Book of Life? By putting your faith in Jesus Christ as your Lord and Savior. No other way. As we read in Acts 4:12, "There is salvation in no one else! There is no other name in all of heaven for people to call on to save them" (NLT). The reference in Revelation 20 to being judged according to our deeds refers to the fact that our deeds reveal whether we are living our faith in the Lord or are living in our selfishness and pride. Our deeds do not save us—they simply reveal our heart.

In this first judgment, God will judge people according to whether or not they had put their faith in Jesus Christ while they were living on earth. Those who professed faith in Christ will be saved. Those who did not believe will be judged and punished.

What about those who have never heard the gospel?
Biblical scholar Leon Morris addresses the question
that inevitably arises: What about those who have never
even heard about God's plan for salvation?

> This is one of the questions about which we are
> indescribably curious, but to which the biblical
> writers do not address themselves. The Bible is a
> practical book; it tells us what we need to know,
> but it does not answer all the questions we can
> think up. But we can say one or two things about
> those who have not heard of God's plan for
> mankind to escape hell's horrors. One is that we
> can be certain that God's wonderful love reaches
> as far as love can reach. Another is that we have
> the example of Cornelius (Acts 10), a man outside
> the recognized people of God but whom God
> called. . . . We do not know what the fate of those
> who have heard the gospel will be. But we do know
> God, and we know that he will do what is right.[2]

I believe that the judgment of those who have never
heard the gospel will be based on the "light" they have
received. For example, God will take into account
whether, like the Jews, a person has the law of Moses
(Romans 2:12) or if he simply has a natural knowledge
of God's moral standards (Romans 2:12-16). One
thing the Bible makes clear is that no one can be declared righteous before God according to his or her
works (Romans 3:19-31). There is no hope for those
who seek to justify themselves at the judgment.

Our only hope. There is hope, however, for those who seek their salvation from God (Romans 2:7). The gospel tells us that God declares us righteous and forgiven, not because of our own works, but because of our trust in Christ. In the death and resurrection of Jesus Christ, God has already acquitted those who believe. God gives us the righteousness of Christ that we could never achieve ourselves. This process is called justification. I once heard someone define justification this way: "It's 'just-as-if-I'd' never sinned."

What this means is that those who have faith in Christ are free from all condemnation (Romans 8:1, 33-39). Those who do not accept Christ will be judged and condemned. The final criterion of judgment is our relation to Christ (see Matthew 10:32-42).

THE SECOND JUDGMENT:
FAITHFULNESS AND FRUITFULNESS

Believers, then, will pass through the first judgment immediately without a threat. But then they face a second judgment. It may be more helpful to use the word "evaluation" to describe this judgment. There is *no condemnation* for those who are in Christ Jesus (Romans 8:1), but there is *evaluation.* Those who put their faith and trust in Christ, whose names are written in the Book of Life, will be evaluated on the basis of what they did with what God gave them. In Matthew 16:27 we read: "The Son of Man is going to come in his Father's glory with his angels, and then he will reward each person according to what he has done."

Our deeds confirm or contradict our faith commitment.
Even as faithfulness in love confirms a marriage vow,
even as integrity in business confirms a contract, so
good deeds confirm faith in Jesus Christ. For some reason, many people seem to have lost sight of the importance of living a life of integrity. Many mistake grace for
a license to do what they want, thinking that because
they are saved by grace there is nothing more they need
to be concerned about. But Jesus says that true faith will
result in a changed life even as a fruit tree naturally pro-
duces fruit (see Matthew 7:15-20).

What fruit is God looking for in our life? There are
at least six things for which you and I will be held accountable when we stand before the Lord. The first is
commitment. The genuineness of our *commitment* to Jesus
Christ will be tested. Matthew 7:21-23 contains some of
the most sobering verses in the Bible.

> Not everyone who says to me, "Lord, Lord," will
> enter the kingdom of heaven, but only he who
> does the will of my Father who is in heaven. Many
> will say to me on that day, "Lord, Lord, did we
> not prophesy in your name, and in your name
> drive out demons and perform many miracles?"
> Then I will tell them plainly, "I never knew you.
> Away from me, you evildoers!"

It is possible to do good things without knowing Jesus
Christ. Those good things will get us nothing. Of first
importance is our relationship with the Lord.

The second point of evaluation is *character*. Does our life exhibit integrity? Has God's Word shaped our values and our behavior? Is our life governed by the Spirit? In 1 Corinthians 6:9-11 Paul writes:

> Do you not know that the wicked will not inherit the kingdom of God? Do not be deceived: Neither the sexually immoral nor idolaters nor adulterers nor male prostitutes nor homosexual offenders nor thieves nor the greedy nor drunkards nor slanderers nor swindlers will inherit the kingdom of God. And that is what some of you were. But you were washed, you were sanctified, you were justified in the name of the Lord Jesus Christ and by the Spirit of our God.

It's important to note that the Greek verb tense used in the quotation from 1 Corinthians indicates a continuing action. In other words, the sins described are not simply occasional slips but are part of a consistent lifestyle. Those who regularly practice such behavior deny genuine faith.

True followers of Christ are not content with questionable character in themselves nor in others. We are to break with anything that compromises the high calling of Christ's disciples. Of course, there are times when we slander, gossip, struggle with greed, and fall prey to innumerable temptations. What then? Will we fail at Judgment Day?

Here's where grace and law are carefully interwoven. As I pointed out in my book *SoulShaping*, I believe that when we fall, we have an opportunity to fall to our knees. We can repent and humble ourselves before the Lord. We can release our sin and once again commit ourselves to obedience. What seems clear to me is this: Whatever we do not release while on the earth we will be forced to face in heaven.[3]

A third quality for which we will be held accountable is *caring*. What is the quality of our love and compassion? We will be evaluated on the basis of the love we've demonstrated in all our relationships. In Matthew 25:41-46, Jesus tells the parable of the sheep and the goats. He describes what will happen at his second coming. After he blesses those who have been faithful and compassionate, he turns to those who have not:

> Then he will say to those on his left, "Depart from me, you who are cursed, into the eternal fire prepared for the devil and his angels. For I was hungry and you gave me nothing to eat, I was thirsty and you gave me nothing to drink, I was a stranger and you did not invite me in, I needed clothes and you did not clothe me, I was sick and in prison and you did not look after me."
>
> They also will answer, "Lord, when did we see you hungry or thirsty or a stranger or needing clothes or sick or in prison, and did not help you?"
>
> He will reply, "I tell you the truth, whatever you did not do for one of the least of these, you did not do for me."
>
> Then they will go away to eternal punishment, but the righteous to eternal life.

You and I will be evaluated on the basis of our caring and our compassion. Again, it isn't a matter of earning our salvation but of demonstrating the reality of Christ's work in and through us. If he is alive in us, it will be clear in how we respond to people in need.

The fourth quality for which we will be accountable is *consecrated service.* How have we used the gifts God has given us? Every one of us has been given talents and gifts to be used for our own joy and for the Lord's service (see 1 Corinthians 12:7). We could view these as God's investment in us. He expects a return—not because he is greedy but because he is eager to have his grace extended in this world. How are you using your gifts, your time, and your economic resources for the kingdom?

The fifth trait by which you and I will be evaluated is our *consistent witness.* In Matthew 5:13-14 Jesus said, "You are the salt of the earth. . . . You are the light of the world." He's telling us that there's no other salt out there, and there's no other light out there. If you're not salting, nobody is! If you're not lighting, nobody is! Are you being a consistent witness? Remember, a witness simply testifies to his or her experience. Some of us need to draw close to God so we can experience him again. We need his touch in our life so we can have an uncompromised witness. In Mark 8:38 Jesus said that if we are ashamed of him, he will be ashamed of us. A hard truth. Jesus calls for an uncompromising witness. He calls for a vital witness. He calls for a consistent witness.

Finally, we will be judged on our *courageous perseverance.* We need courageous perseverance to hang on to the

Lord, even when everyone else is turning against us, even when we are faced with persecution.

How do you think you will be evaluated in the second judgment?

Are you demonstrating a genuine commitment to Jesus Christ?

Are you pursuing a character that honors him?

Are you caring for others, especially "the least," in practical ways?

Are you using your gifts in consecrated service to the Lord?

Are you a consistent witness for Christ?

Do you show courageous perseverance in the face of stress and even persecution?

The hope of our heavenly inheritance inspires us to lead a godly life, a life that models the qualities of Jesus moment by moment. And as a result, in the second judgment we may receive rewards based on the fruit of faith in our life.

WE WILL ALL RECEIVE AN INHERITANCE

When we have passed through judgment, we will receive our inheritance. An inheritance is not the same thing as a reward. Our inheritance is unearned. Our reward will be a gracious recognition of faithfulness.

Let's look first at our inheritance. According to 1 Peter 1:3-6, you and I are to rejoice *now* because of the inheritance that awaits us in heaven.

Praise be to the God and Father of our Lord
Jesus Christ! In his great mercy he has given
us new birth into a living hope through the
resurrection of Jesus Christ from the dead, and
into an inheritance that can never perish, spoil
or fade—kept in heaven for you, who through
faith are shielded by God's power until the
coming of the salvation that is ready to be
revealed in the last time. In this you greatly
rejoice, though now for a little while you may
have had to suffer grief in all kinds of trials.

Peter is making the point that *we can no more earn our
heavenly inheritance than we can earn our birth.* If you understand this concept, it will change your view of Christianity. You can no more earn heaven than you can earn
your birth. Circumstances totally beyond your control
resulted in your being born. Likewise you did nothing
to be born again. This is stated most clearly in Ephesians 2:1-5:

As for you, you were dead in your transgressions
and sins, in which you used to live when you
followed the ways of this world and of the ruler
of the kingdom of the air, the spirit who is now
at work in those who are disobedient. All of us
also lived among them at one time, gratifying the
cravings of our sinful nature and following its
desires and thoughts. Like the rest, we were by
nature objects of wrath. But because of his great
love for us, God, who is rich in mercy, made us

alive with Christ even when we were dead in transgressions—it is by grace you have been saved.

If you have already turned to faith in Jesus Christ, it's because the grace of God has awakened your heart. If that hasn't happened for you but you long for it, the Holy Spirit is stirring your heart right now.

Just as you did nothing to earn your spiritual birth, you don't have to do anything to earn your spiritual inheritance. In the normal course of things, you receive an inheritance simply because you're a member of a family. Whatever inheritance awaits you from your earthly relatives comes your way totally unearned.

The wonder of the gospel is this: We who believe are *joint heirs* with Jesus Christ (see Romans 8:17). To grasp the meaning of this, imagine getting a call from a lawyer saying the wealthiest person in the world has just died, leaving you an equal share in his estate with his children! You've been made a joint heir. Would that get your attention? It would be great, wouldn't it? Greater still—infinitely greater—is the fact that you are a joint heir with Jesus Christ.

It's difficult to imagine what our inheritance will be like, but the apostle Peter gives us several descriptions.

OUR INHERITANCE IS IMPERISHABLE

Living in an agricultural area has helped me appreciate the incredible challenge farmers have in getting their produce to market before it perishes. If the produce wilts or spoils, all is lost. Our heavenly inheritance, on the other hand, isn't time sensitive. It won't spoil. It's imperishable. Moth and rust don't consume it. It isn't subject to the processes and limitations of finite time.

OUR INHERITANCE IS PURE

Unlike every other earthly thing, our inheritance is undefiled. This means it is untouched by evil. Untainted by sin. Unpolluted by evil thought or association. When you receive your inheritance, it will be pure—as pure a pleasure, as pure a gift, as pure an experience as you can ever imagine.

OUR INHERITANCE IS UNFADING

The joys and satisfactions of our inheritance will not dim throughout eternity. There are countless possessions and experiences in our life whose initial splendors fade. Marriages move from the honeymoon stage to the challenges, stresses, and strains of life together. Paint jobs peel. Fabrics deteriorate. Machinery breaks or wears out. Flower blossoms bloom and die. But in heaven, the joys, beauties, and pleasures will go on and on and on.

Peter tells us all these things are kept for us. The Greek concept here could be compared to a financial trust. In economic terms, if something has been held in trust for you, it is kept until you reach maturity or fulfill the conditions of the trust. Likewise, your heavenly inheritance is already yours, held in trust for you. In fact, the Holy Spirit is God's deposit guaranteeing that the heavenly trust will be yours forever (see Ephesians 1:14)! Now wouldn't you expect it to be the other way around? It seems to me we should put some sort of deposit down on heaven. Yet God has given us a deposit instead.

Amazing! So the first thing to realize is that we already have an inheritance if we have put our faith and trust in Jesus Christ. It is pure, it is undefiled, it is unfading, it is imperishable, and it is waiting for you and for me.

WHAT ABOUT REWARDS?

The Bible says there will be rewards in heaven. While all who believe in the Lord will live in heaven, there seem to be different stations of heaven and different rewards. For instance, using the image of building, Paul speaks of the rewards that we may receive for being a faithful disciple.

> For no one can lay any foundation other than the one already laid, which is Jesus Christ. If any man builds on this foundation using gold, silver, costly stones, wood, hay, or straw, his work will be shown for what it is, because the Day will bring it to light. It will be revealed with fire, and the fire will test the quality of each man's work. If what he has built survives, he will receive his reward. If it is burned up, he will suffer loss; he himself will be saved, but only as one escaping through the flames. (1 Corinthians 3:11-15)

We will examine these words more closely in a moment, but first we need to make sense of trusting in God's grace and receiving a reward. If we don't think carefully, we will replace grace with good works.

Our heavenly reward simply will be a recognition of

ur faithfulness in response to God's gift. We can understand this more clearly through an analogy with the Special Olympics. The Special Olympics is an international program of training and athletic competition for people with mental retardation. This program was founded in 1968 by Eunice Kennedy Shriver, sister of former president John F. Kennedy. The program serves nearly one million athletes in more than 140 countries. The hallmark of the Special Olympics is the equal emphasis placed on both training and competitions. This is seen most clearly in supporters who are called "huggers." They literally hug Special Olympics participants, encouraging them in every way possible. Participants are rewarded for participation, not for competition. They are rewarded for doing what they can, realizing that they did it with a whole lot of support. Everybody wins! The goal isn't a world record but helping each person reach farther than he or she may have ever thought possible.

How would you respond if I told you that the same principle—of reward for participation, not competition—applies in the Christian life? Would you be surprised if I said that we are all in the heavenly Special Olympics? Here's what I mean: I am absolutely incapable of achieving perfection in following Jesus Christ. Left to my own devices, I will stumble. I am, spiritually speaking, disabled by sin. I will do wrong. But by the power of his Holy Spirit, by the guidance of his Word, by the encouragement of God's people, I'm getting through. I'm not setting any world records. But God will recognize me for faithfulness, faithfulness that is possible only because of God's help.

There will be no strutting in heaven. The rewards we receive will be the gracious gift of God's grace in recognition of our faithfulness to his promises, of our trust in his provision, of our joy in his service, and of our experience of his goodness.

THE CROWNS OF BLESSING

The Bible describes our heavenly rewards as "crowns." There are five crowns listed in the Bible that may be given to faithful followers of Christ. The interpretation of these crowns should not be pressed too far. The following comments are simply meant to suggest some of the rich possibilities that await us in God's grace.

The crown of life. James 1:12 says that we will receive a "crown of life." This is the crown we receive when we pass through trials and remain faithful. When we live with heaven in mind, we don't live for the immediate reward—which often comes at the cost of compromising our faith or our moral standards. Instead, we endure pressure, punishment, even persecution because of the hope of receiving eternal life with the Lord. The promise of the crown of life keeps us looking beyond the trials of this earthly life to the victory and joy that will be ours in Christ.

The crown of righteousness. This crown is spoken of in the context of finishing well, of persevering. At the end of his life, Paul wrote, "For I am already being poured out like a drink offering, and the time has come for my departure. I have fought the good fight, I have finished the race, I have kept the faith. Now there is in store for me the crown of righteousness, which the Lord, the righteous Judge, will award to me on that day—and not only to me, but also to all who have longed for his appearing" (2 Timothy 4:6-8).

There is value in maintaining integrity over the long journey of life. Nothing matters much more than finishing well. King David started well, didn't he? How did he finish? Not well. The consequences of his sin with Bathsheba never left him. He was forgiven, but there was conflict in his household for the rest of his life. For those who don't fall—or who get up, seek forgiveness, and move forward in integrity—there is a crown of righteousness in heaven.

The crown of incorruptibility. The prize for winning an Olympic contest used to be a crownlike laurel wreath. Paul writes about athletes who work hard for a perishable crown:

> Do you not know that in a race all the runners run, but only one gets the prize? Run in such a way as to get the prize. Everyone who competes in the games goes into strict training. They do it to get a crown that will not last; but we do it to get a crown that will last forever. Therefore I do not run like a man running aimlessly; I do not fight like a man beating the air. No, I beat my body and make it my slave so that after I have preached

to others, I myself will not be disqualified for the prize. (1 Corinthians 9:24-27)

The much-sought-after Olympic wreath would fade. Its leaves would become brittle and drop off. But our heavenly crown will be incorruptible. Our heavenly reward will neither fade nor dim. All that we receive will endure; it will not be subject to forces of decay.

Are you investing in things that will last? Have you thought about what will last? What it really comes down to is people. Whatever you're doing in life, you can find a way to build the people around you in the process. That's extending the kingdom of God.

The crown of rejoicing. In 1 Thessalonians 2:19-20, Paul says that those who have come to know Jesus Christ are his greatest reason for joy. God will crown Paul because he was faithful in proclaiming the Good News. The crown of rejoicing is the evangelist's crown. Are you living as a witness? Is there someone in the world who can say, "I know more about Jesus because of you"? If so, you'll receive a crown of rejoicing in heaven.

The crown of glory. First Peter 5:2-4 speaks of the crown that God gives in recognition of faithful service: "Be shepherds of God's flock that is under your care, serving as overseers—not because you must, but because you are willing, as God wants you to be; not greedy for money, but eager to serve; not lording it over those entrusted to you, but being examples to the flock. And when the Chief Shepherd appears, you will receive the crown of glory that will never fade away."

This passage is addressed to all who serve, whether lay people or ordained clergy. God says, in effect, "I will recognize your invisible hours. I will recognize the secret burdens that you carry because you are active in my service. I will repay you for all you paid. Your service will be evident to all through a crown of glory."

WHAT WILL WE DO WITH OUR CROWNS?

You're likely to use your time more wisely, control your desires more strictly, invest your abilities more effectively, and keep your priorities more diligently if you remember that you will have to give an account to God—and that you're going to get a reward in heaven. But when you get your heavenly crown (or maybe you'll get all five crowns!), you're not going to wear it very long. Revelation 4:9-11 offers a beautiful image of worship around the throne:

> Whenever the living creatures give glory, honor and thanks to him who sits on the throne and who lives for ever and ever, the twenty-four elders fall down before him who sits on the throne, and worship him who lives for ever and ever. They lay their crowns before the throne and say:
>
> > "You are worthy, our Lord and God,
> > to receive glory and honor and power,
> > for you created all things,
> > and by your will they were created
> > and have their being."

When you get to heaven and God gives you a crown, you're going to say, "That's wonderful, Lord, but it really belongs to you!" And you will lay it before him, along with the innumerable crowns that others have laid there, too.

WONDERFUL AS THEY ARE, OUR CROWNS ARE NOTHING TO BOAST ABOUT

First Corinthians 1:31 says, "Let him who boasts boast in the Lord." Boast in the Lord, who gave Jesus Christ to die in your place. Boast in the Lord, who sent someone to tell you the good news of the gospel. Boast in Lord, who gave you ears to hear and a heart to respond. Boast in the Lord, who gave you a place where your faith could be nurtured and where you could be encouraged. Boast in Lord, who gave you abilities that you could use in ways that bring you satisfaction while you bring glory to him. Boast in the Lord, who gives you a measure of health so that you can serve him. Boast in the Lord, who gives you favor with people who will welcome your service. Boast in the Lord, who gives you opportunities, networks, connections, and experiences, all of which come together in a way that you never could have orchestrated.

What else do you have to boast in? Nothing. So I encourage you: Rejoice in the inheritance that is yours. Lead a life that bears fruit in faithfulness, commitment, and consecrated service. This is the fruit that brings glory to God. Wear his name in an honorable way, and he will reward you.

The Bible says that we will all be judged. The first

judgment will separate those who have placed their faith in Christ from those who haven't, those who have been freed from condemnation from those who are condemned. The second judgment, an evaluation of believers, will hold us accountable for the way we have lived our life. Showing our life to God is a sobering prospect but also a hopeful one, because we are promised both an inheritance and a reward. The hope of inheritance and the hope of reward inspire us to lead a godly life. May we look to the Lord to cleanse us of our failures and to empower our obedience.

NOTES

1. "Parables of Judgment and the Future," *Student's Life Application Bible* (Wheaton, Ill.: Tyndale House Publishers, Inc., 1997), p. 1349.

2. Leon Morris, "Hell: The Dreadful Harvest," *Christianity Today* (27 May 1991): 37.

3. Douglas J. Rumford, *SoulShaping* (Wheaton, Ill.: Tyndale House Publishers, Inc., 1996), 420.

CHAPTER FOUR

"How Can You Say There's a Hell?"

During college a group of us were doing a religious survey as a means to discuss faith with strangers. My partner, Dan, went up to one middle-aged man and asked if he'd be willing to take the survey. It immediately became obvious that this man had been approached before.

"I suppose you're going to ask me if I'm saved," said the man. "Well, I have a question for you: Saved from what? Don't tell me you really believe in hell! That went out with the Middle Ages!"

Some people find it offensive to bring up the topic of hell, which is curious since we live in a time when many truly offensive subjects are out in the open. People talk publicly about sexuality and bodily functions in the most intimate and embarrassing detail but flinch at the mention of hell. I must admit that I don't like hell either. I preach and write about it primarily out of obedience and faithfulness, like the doctor who has to tell a patient bad news. Confidence in the truth of God's

Word and his love for people forces me to speak of things no one wants to talk about.

Hell is certainly out of fashion. In an age of "tolerance," it represents the ultimate intolerance. Hell, by its very definition, means someone is wrong and will suffer the consequences of his or her error. In the name of tolerance, we are tempted to sacrifice the hard edge of truth for the soft comfort of sentimentality. We are in danger of leaving the solid ground of objective truth and falling into the quicksand of subjectivism. If everybody's opinion is equally valid, we will wallow in confusion. But that is not the true meaning of tolerance. The true meaning of tolerance lies in our respect for people, not in denial of truth. We can love people without agreeing with them. We can respect people without agreeing that their "truth" is as valid as any other "truth." We do not have the license to despise people because of their beliefs or opinions. But that does not mean that their opinions have equal truth value. People can be sincerely wrong. And when it comes to hell, resting on opinions can be especially precarious. Because many people do not truly believe in the horror of hell, they don't see an urgent need for Jesus Christ. So it's important to understand why some people don't believe in hell.

IT'S HARD TO BELIEVE IN HELL BECAUSE IT SEEMS TO CONTRADICT THE PRINCIPLE OF LOVE

People say, "How can you tell me that a loving God is going to send someone to hell?" Their logic goes like this: *Love never hurts anyone. God is love. Therefore, God would never hurt anyone, especially by sending them to hell.* The problem with this logic is that it's based on a false definition of love.

SEDUCED BY THE ILLUSION OF SENTIMENTAL LOVE

What I just described is a sentimental love, not the kind of love portrayed in the Bible. Sentimental love is based on feeling. It doesn't let another person get hurt. Psychologists have helped us understand that sentimental love is actually destructive. People who won't let others get hurt or suffer as a consequence of their actions are actually harming them by removing responsibility from them. This is often called enabling or codependent behavior. For example, what happens if a child comes home with an F on his report card? In a healthy home, the parents take steps to understand the failure and encourage the child to take responsibility for improving his grades. They may institute punishments, restrictions, summer school, tutors, or any number of other means, but ultimately the child is responsible. In a codependent situation, the parent would call the teacher and say, "My child is not an 'F' child! There must be some mistake. I expect there to be a way to change that grade, or else I'm going to the principal." The parent in this situation is behaving in an irresponsible way, protecting the child and trying to remove the consequence of failing behavior. The problem is that children have to learn the consequences of their behavior, or they will become more and more irresponsible.

Another common situation in which people confuse

real love with sentimental love is when there is an alcoholic spouse in a marriage. Often the nonalcoholic spouse will cover up for the alcoholic. When the alcoholic is so drunk or hung over that he misses work, the spouse calls in and says, "I'm sorry, he's really sick today. He'll be in tomorrow." But studies have shown that until the nonalcoholic spouse shows tough love, change will never happen. Until the spouse says, *"You* will have to call your boss, because I refuse to," the alcoholic won't begin to think about taking responsibility. Tough love is real love. It is a love that honors and respects all the people involved, letting responsibility fall where it belongs.

Many people's sentimental view of God's love leads them to believe that he wouldn't allow humans to experience the consequences of their choices. Such a view has no basis in Scripture. God's great love for us is tough love.

TAKING FREEDOM SERIOUSLY

God takes our freedom seriously. But we must realize that freedom has a dark side. The freedom to speed in an automobile means the possibility of a traffic ticket—or worse, an accident. The freedom to choose means the possibility of making a wrong choice. Freedom carries within it the seeds of consequences that will sprout either into a harvest of joy or a plague of weed-like problems.

God created humanity with the freedom to choose. But inherent in that freedom is the possibility of judgment and death. Among other things, we were created

with the freedom to reject God. But there are consequences in that rejection. The problem is that we want
freedom without consequences. In other words, we
want the equivalent of diet caffeine-free cola. No calories, no caffeine—taste without consequences! But life
isn't like that soda. To shift metaphors, we can't eat the
cake of sin without getting the calories of consequences!

One of the Bible's most vivid stories about the freedom to choose or reject God is Jesus' encounter with
the rich young ruler, who asked him what he needed to
do to get into heaven:

> Jesus felt genuine love for this man as he looked
> at him. "You lack only one thing," he told him.
> "Go and sell all you have and give the money to
> the poor, and you will have treasure in heaven.
> Then come, follow me." At this, the man's face
> fell, and he went sadly away because he had many
> possessions. (Mark 10:21-22, NLT)

The most surprising feature of this story is the fact
that Jesus let the young man walk away. To me, that is
absolutely astounding. I would have been tempted to
lower the requirements, to reduce the demands, to coax
the young man to meet me halfway. But God doesn't
negotiate.

We must not mistake the comfort and support of love
for a willingness to excuse careless liberties and license.
Love welcomes and comforts all who respect it. But love
does not tolerate disrespect and irresponsibility. I
heard someone say that love will always excuse a blind

person who steps on its toes but will back away from a person who continually tries to stomp on it. Love may not keep a record of wrongs, but it does discern the nature of those wrongs. If they arise from willful disregard and cavalier selfishness, love quickly steps back. Even what we call unconditional love has one essential condition: that each person in the relationship accept an appropriate level of responsibility.

Hell, then, is the natural consequence of freedom and love, a fulfillment of justice. If justice rewards those who respect the order of things, then justice demands a penalty for those who don't.

See the irony! Some demand their freedom and then, when things turn out wrong, complain to God, "Wait a minute! How could you let this happen?" We tread on very thin ice when we demand that God has to set us free to do what we please—and then insist that he has to protect us from the consequences. I don't know what that is, but it isn't love.

We are tempted to try to create God in our own image, after our own liking. Thomas Jefferson, second president of the United States and primary author of the Declaration of Independence, developed his own version of the Bible. He copied our Bible but eliminated all references to the supernatural and selected only the moral teachings of Jesus. The closing words of Jefferson's Bible are: "There laid they Jesus and rolled a great stone at the mouth of the sepulchre and departed."[1] While we may respect his political savvy, we must not imitate Thomas Jefferson's theology. We don't have the privilege of editing the Bible! It is not a loose-leaf document that can be expanded or deleted according to human preference or whim. It is the Word of God—and it teaches that a loving God gave us freedom to reject him, a freedom that has eternal consequences.

IT IS HARD TO BELIEVE IN HELL BECAUSE WE THINK GOD EXPECTS TOO MUCH OF US

Even if we accept the legitimacy of consequences, we are inclined to resist the concept of hell: After all, how can there be eternal consequences for what we do in such a short lifetime?

God expects one of two things from human beings: absolute perfection or else a clear admission of failure and acceptance of his solution to our problem. Either would be acceptable. But God doesn't compromise his standards. We either fulfill them ourselves or rely on his way of fulfilling them. God doesn't grade on a curve.

We may be able to understand and even accept the judgment of hell for a person who deliberately defies God or is a practicing atheist or a mass murderer. Some people's conduct is so despicable that we can believe they deserve the terror of hell for the torment they have brought to others. But we may struggle with the assertion that ordinary, everyday people are going to hell. After all, they aren't really that bad.

This view fails to recognize that the severity of wrongdoing is measured in part by the stature of the one against whom the wrong has been committed. Our language system recognizes the difference between murder and assassination. In both cases, a person dies. But the grievousness of the crime is considered in proportion to the victim's place in the society as a whole. Thus the punishment for assassinating a public official may be different from that for murdering an average citizen.

Now the question is this: What is God worth? And what is the appropriate punishment for one who defies God, who spurns God's love, who refuses to fulfill his or her duty to God? Jonathan Edwards writes:

> The crime of one being despising and casting contempt on another is proportionably more or less heinous, as he was under greater or less obligation to obey him. And therefore if there be any being that we are under infinite obligations to love, and honor, and obey, the contrary towards him must be infinitely faulty. . . . So sin against God, being a violation of infinite obligations, must be a crime infinitely heinous, and so deserving infinite punishment.[2]

God is infinitely worthy of everything we have: our money, heart, home, talents, and gifts. But if we snub God, who is worthy of all, does it make sense that there would be no consequences? Hell is just, because God has a legitimate claim on each of us.

Still, some would say that if a person just had more time, he or she would eventually believe in God. Let's consider that. What would more years do for a person who has chosen to ignore God? Think of a garden. If you ignore your garden for months, what happens? Instead of a garden, you have a weed patch! That's what happens with the spiritual life. If you ignore it for months, it won't suddenly blossom into glorious praises to God. If you ignore God, your heart will go to weeds. *A life left to itself will leave God.* It's a mistake to think that time has anything to do with the orientation of the heart.

We may acknowledge that love means allowing people freedom to choose and to suffer the consequences of their choices. And we may concede that God has every right to expect to be treated with respect and honor. But we may still find it hard to believe in hell because we can't imagine that Jesus really believed in it. But some of the clearest teaching available to us about hell came from Jesus.

JESUS TAUGHT THE REALITY OF HELL

People have said to me, "I can't believe in hell because Jesus taught about love and accepting everybody, no matter what they do." My response is one question: "Which Bible are you reading?"

Check out the Gospel of Matthew. It reveals ample evidence that hell was one of Jesus' primary concerns. In Matthew 5–7, known commonly as the Sermon on the Mount, Jesus gives vivid warnings about the consequences of sin:

> You have heard that it was said to the people long ago, "Do not murder, and anyone who murders

will be subject to judgment." But I tell you that anyone who is angry with his brother will be subject to judgment. Again, anyone who says to his brother, "Raca," is answerable to the Sanhedrin. But anyone who says, "You fool!" will be in danger of the fire of hell. (Matthew 5:21-22)

He gives a similar warning concerning lust and adultery:

If your right eye causes you to sin, gouge it out and throw it away. It is better for you to lose one part of your body than for your whole body to be thrown into hell. And if your right hand causes you to sin, cut it off and throw it away. It is better for you to lose one part of your body than for your whole body to go into hell. (Matthew 5:29-30)

Jesus took hell very seriously. In Matthew 8:11-12 (NLT) he says, "And I tell you this, that many Gentiles will come from all over the world and sit down with Abraham, Isaac, and Jacob at the feast in the Kingdom of Heaven. But many Israelites—those for whom the Kingdom was prepared—will be cast into outer darkness, where there will be weeping and gnashing of teeth." Matthew 25 talks about separating the sheep from the goats. It's a picture a lot like that of Jesus' parable about the rich man and Lazarus (see Luke 16:19-31). Those who failed to take care of the needy are contrasted with those who did. At the end of the chapter, the people who failed and are on their way to hell say, "'Lord, when did we see you hungry or thirsty or a stranger or needing clothes or sick or in prison, and did not help you?' He will reply, 'I tell you the truth, whatever you did not do for one of the least of these, you did not do for me.' Then they will go away to eternal punishment" (Matthew 25:44-46). Those whose say Jesus never taught about hell reveal their own ignorance.

The best-known verse of all time, John 3:16, says, "For God so loved the world, that he gave his only begotten Son, that whosoever believeth in him should not perish, but have everlasting life" (KJV). According to that verse, is perishing a possibility? Yes! To perish basically means to go to hell, to be eternally separated from God. (We'll see more clearly what hell is like in the next chapter.)

LIFE MAKES NO SENSE UNLESS HELL EXISTS

As difficult a concept as hell is to confront, I believe in it because without it, nothing else makes sense.

HELL IS CONSISTENT WITH THE REALITY OF EVIL

Perhaps you have heard this old story:

> A scorpion and a frog were at the edge of a river. The river was at flood stage, and the scorpion, who was unable to swim, wanted to get to the other side. So he said to the frog, "Mr. Frog, may I hop on your back to ride across the river?"
> The frog said, "How could you ask such a

thing? You're a scorpion! Everyone knows you could sting me and kill me!"

"Oh, Mr. Frog, I know you've heard such things about us scorpions in the past, but we are living in more enlightened times now. We are not barbaric killers. I wouldn't sting you. I need you. Besides, I can keep you company on that long journey across the river. Won't you please take me over?"

The frog thought for a few moments. "No, I just can't do it. My mom always told me, 'Watch out for scorpions.'"

"But Mr. Frog, when are you going to learn to think for yourself? Your mom might have been right in the old days, I know. Some of my parents and grandparents—well, frankly, I can't help what they were like. But I assure you, things are different now. I won't hurt you."

Finally the frog agreed and let the scorpion on his back. As they crossed the river the scorpion chitchatted the whole way. But when they got to the other side, the scorpion stung the frog and then hopped off. The frog felt the poison burning through his veins. Realizing he was about to die, he cried out, "You lied to me! What did you do that for?"

The scorpion replied simply, "Don't you know—some things never change?"

Evil is evil is evil—and that will never change. If you mess with scorpions, you're going to get stung. The person who chooses evil over God will be stung by the consequences of evil.

Hell Fulfills the Demands of Justice

As with heaven, the existence of hell fits not only with the clear teaching of the Bible but with our own instincts and intuition—which tell us that wrong must be punished, that evil must not have the last word. We know in our heart that for justice to be served, evil must be punished.

I was speaking at a men's Bible study about our innate sense of morality. One of the men said, "But Doug, other cultures have totally different definitions of morality, of what is right and wrong. How can we be certain there is any 'standard' morality?"

An idea suddenly hit me, and I said, "The moral sense is like our capacity for language. We may speak different languages, but we are admitting the reality and capacity and value of language simply by speaking. One person may use language to curse, while another uses it to bless. That's the way it is with morality and accountability. Even as we have 'eternity in our heart,' so also we have an innate moral sense. The vast majority of people have a strong sense of right and wrong, of fairness and justice, even if they don't agree on specifics. This is inherent to human nature and seems to be part of the fabric of the universe."

Our innate sense of morality tells us that evil must be punished. To ignore hell, to distort it, to downplay it, to arrogantly dismiss it, is to dance where angels will only tiptoe.

HELL EXPLAINS THE NECESSITY OF CHRIST'S BIRTH AND DEATH

If hell isn't real, why did Jesus Christ come to earth and walk among us? To get away from heaven? Somehow I don't think the manger looked that good! Jesus came precisely because we were condemned to hell unless he did something about it. According to John 3:17, those who do not believe are condemned already. If God's wrath were no big deal, why was Jesus so concerned about it?

If hell is not real, there is one question I can never answer, one huge problem I can never resolve. Let me put it very directly: If there is no hell, why the Cross? This is the ultimate question.

Put this book aside for a few moments and reflect on that question: *If there is no hell, why the Cross?* Why would Jesus die if there were no need to rescue us from a dreadful destiny? If you have any doubt how serious this matter is, you need only reflect on the fact that Jesus was willing to be crucified so you and I could escape hell.

Jesus Christ believed hell was so serious that he gave his life so that you and I wouldn't have to go there. Those who reject Jesus must accept the consequences.

As I said at the beginning, we must not sacrifice the hard edge of truth on the altar of soft, comfortable sentimentality. We've lost the urgency of the gospel in our day because we've lost the reality of hell. Without hell, the gospel makes no sense. Without hell, there is no grace.

MORE THAN AN INTELLECTUAL QUESTION

While the subject of heaven and hell is fascinating, it is much more than an interesting topic of conversation. It is literally a matter of life and death. Whenever I reflect on it, I am overwhelmed by the implications. We dare not take the subject lightly. As the Bible says, "Today, if you hear his voice, do not harden your hearts" (Hebrews 3:7).

I was talking recently with a businessperson whose employee was caught using the Internet to access pornography during office hours. The employee saw nothing wrong with using pornography, going so far as to say that it was a matter of personal privacy. The employer considered all the ramifications of the situation, including the company's specific policy prohibiting the use of company computers for pornography, and finally concluded that the employee needed to be terminated. Of course, the supervisor suggested all manner of help and provided severance benefits, but the bottom line was that the employee's actions cost him his job. Not all things are tolerable.

Our choices have consequences not only in this life but also in the next. Failing to proclaim the bad news of hell leaves people with a false sense of security and distorted values for living. Someday there will be a surprise—a tragic surprise.

NOTES

1. Adapted from Paul Lee Tan, *Encyclopedia of 7700 Illustrations* (Rockville, Md.: Assurance Publishers, 1979), 669.

2. Jonathan Edwards, "The Justice of God in the Damnation of Sinners," *The Works of Jonathan Edwards,* vol. 1 (Edinburgh: Banner of Truth Trust, 1974), 669. Quoted in John Piper, *Desiring God* (Portland: Multnomah Press, 1986), 46.

CHAPTER FIVE

"What Is Hell Like?"

The headline of a newspaper article caught my attention. It read "It May Be Harder to Get to Hell This Year."

> It may be harder to get to Hell this year. A bridge on the main road leading to Hell, Michigan, is badly in need of repair, a project that could close the road for three months. Business owners in the town fear that the disruption in traffic would force some stores into bankruptcy. "It'll close the whole town," complained Jim Lee, the President of the Hell Chamber of Commerce. Officials acknowledged that the repair work will cause some disruption but insist that the plans to fix the road to Hell are paved with good intentions. The road has suffered great damage each time Hell freezes over.[1]

Unless we're talking about a town in Michigan, the Bible says it's all too easy to get to hell. But most people ignore that headline. Failing to proclaim the bad news of hell leaves people with a false sense of security and distorted values. They are traveling down a road that leads to a literal dead end. Hell is serious business!

IS HELL JUST A SCARE TACTIC?

Many people assert that hell is just a tactic used to scare and manipulate people, to coerce the weak-minded into believing in God. In truth, there have been times in the history of Christianity when fear was used to try to force people to faith. But the plain fact is that we talk about hell because the Bible asserts that hell is a reality. And if hell is as the Bible describes it, no more frightening a reality exists.

Imagine a physician who tells a patient who smokes about the experience of people who get lung cancer and emphysema. He describes their shortness of breath, their feeling of being choked, the ordeal of treatment. But the patient responds, "Come off it, Doc! You're just trying to scare me." He fails to realize that the doctor's goal isn't fear—it's life! The physician isn't trying to generate cringing terror but to motivate practical, life-enhancing change.

It's hard to talk about hell. My goal isn't to scare anybody but to present, as clearly as I know how, the dangers that lie ahead for those who refuse the way of faith. I want people to be drawn to heaven by love, but they cannot see the value of Jesus' love without an understanding of the terrifying doom from which God is willing to rescue them. By God's grace, if the warning signs are read early enough, people will choose another road.

What is hell like? The Bible actually has relatively few passages containing specific descriptions of it. If you look in the Bible for pictures of heaven, you can just open the book of Revelation. Glorious images of heaven are revealed: the gates of pearl, the streets of gold, and more important, the presence of God, wiping away every tear from our eyes. The pictures are quite vivid. But the Bible doesn't give us much detail about hell. We must be careful about speculating over issues about which the Bible is silent. Our beliefs must not go beyond God's revelation. So what *does* the Bible say about hell?

IN HELL, PEOPLE EXPERIENCE THE FULL JUDGMENT AGAINST SIN

We do not suffer the full consequences of our actions in this life. We do not see the full impact of our sin in God's eyes. We do not fully see how much we violate ourselves. We do not fully see how much we hurt people. We do not fully see how future generations will be affected by our actions. But every once in a while, we catch a dreadful glimpse.

WHAT JUST A GLIMPSE OF JUDGMENT TELLS US

As I was writing the first draft of this book, the United States was being subjected to the scandal of President Bill Clinton and White House intern Monica Lewinsky. Clinton's improper conduct with Ms. Lewinsky and subsequent testimony under oath led all the way to an impeachment trial in the United States Senate—something that had happened only one other time in the nation's 220-year-old history. The lurid details of their behavior was described in newspapers and magazines, on television, radio, and the Internet. Regardless of people's political views, most were disgusted by the conduct of the president and Ms. Lewinsky. The two of them were humiliated. It's hard to imagine the degree of their embarrassment.

In this scandal two people were forced to face the consequences of their actions. Can you imagine if that happened to you? What if some of the things you've done in secret were broadcast in public? Think of the humiliation and shame you'd feel. That, I believe, would be just a glimpse of what hell is like. In this world, more often than not, we forget, we deny, we hide, or we just plain don't get it. We don't experience the full consequences of our actions. But someday we will.

My wife, Sarah, and I were on a marriage retreat during which the speaker had us go to our room and write a list of all of our sins against our spouse. Then we were to confess them and ask forgiveness. I'll confess right now that I did not want to do this! But I gave in, prayed for wisdom and courage—and started writing. I was surprised by the first thing that came to mind. Later, I read Sarah the sin that emerged at the top of the list. "Sarah," I said, "I confess that I have devalued your church and your hometown." I loved the people of her church and enjoyed her hometown, but I suddenly realized that I had sometimes conveyed a tone, often simply through innuendo, that my larger church and hometown were better. Up to this point in the marriage exercise, Sarah had been playful and casual. But when I confessed this sin, I watched her playful smile disappear and tears come down her cheeks.

And then she said to me, very softly, "You really did devalue things that were important to me."

I only caught a little glimpse of the way my behavior had wounded my wife. Just a tiny glimpse. And it was devastating to me.

I got a glimpse of the effects of my wrong behavior, but most of us never see sin in its full ramifications. Rarely does the perpetrator of a crime have to sit with the victim of that crime face-to-face and hear his or her emotional pain. Perhaps there is a general mercy that shields us from understanding the full consequences of our sin. Undoubtedly, there are also countless defense mechanisms we use to avoid facing our sin. But if we reject Jesus, the day will come when we will experience sin's full impact.

IN HELL, THERE IS NO GRACE

The message of the Bible is clear: Those who seem to be "getting away with" ungodliness will one day face the consequences. Second Peter 2 gives a sobering overview of God's judgment:

> For God did not spare even the angels when they sinned; he threw them into hell, in gloomy caves and darkness until the judgment day. And God did not spare the ancient world—except for

Noah and his family of seven. Noah warned the world of God's righteous judgment. Then God destroyed the whole world of ungodly people with a vast flood. Later, he turned the cities of Sodom and Gomorrah into heaps of ashes and swept them off the face of the earth. He made them an example of what will happen to ungodly people. But at the same time, God rescued Lot out of Sodom because he was a good man who was sick of all the immorality and wickedness around him. Yes, he was a righteous man who was distressed by the wickedness he saw and heard day after day.

So you see, the Lord knows how to rescue godly people from their trials, even while punishing the wicked right up until the day of judgment. He is especially hard on those who follow their own evil, lustful desires and who despise authority. These people are proud and arrogant, daring even to scoff at the glorious ones without so much as trembling. But the angels, even though they are far greater in power and strength than these false teachers, never speak out disrespectfully against the glorious ones. (2 Peter 2:4-11, NLT)

Even in this passage on judgment, the message of grace shines through—but only for those who are willing to accept it during this life. God judged the world but, by his grace, saved Noah. God judged Sodom and Gomorrah but, by his grace, saved Lot. Clearly, God knows how to rescue the righteous. In the midst of the message of condemnation, there is the reminder of God's rescuing power. God has done everything necessary to cover our sin, to welcome us back to himself. In the midst of the bad news, remember his grace—but realize also that there is no grace in hell. None whatsoever.

THE HELL OF REMEMBERING

Dwight L. Moody was preaching a sermon on hell and was greatly intrigued by Jesus' description of it as a place "where their worm dieth not, and the fire is not quenched" (Mark 9:44, KJV). Moody wrote:

> The Spirit of God tells us that we shall carry our memory with us into the other world. There are many things we would like to forget. . . . I believe the worm that dieth not is our memory. We say now that we forget and we think we do, but the time is coming when we shall remember and cannot forget. We talk about the recording angel keeping a record of our life. God makes us keep our own record. We won't need anyone to condemn us at the bar (or the court) of God. It will be our own conscience that will come as a witness against us. God won't condemn us at his bar or court, we shall condemn ourselves. Memory is God's officer, and when he shall touch these secret springs and say, "Son, Daughter, remember"—then tramp, tramp, tramp, will come before us, in a long procession, all the sins we have ever committed.[2]

Does that description send you reeling? It does me! I remember watching a film in a high school biology class about a science experiment in which physicians used electronic probes to determine the neurology of the brain. When probing in the "memory section" of one woman's brain, they asked her to tell them how many telephone poles she passed by on her way to work. Normally, of course, none of us could answer such a question. But this woman could literally remember every detail of the road—and could count the poles as if she were actually driving to work! In other words, our mind has recorded much more than we consciously remember.

Hell broils with grief and regret, fueled by the memories of this life. Have you ever had that "morning-after" feeling, when you wake up remembering with embarrassment and regret something you did the day or night before? Hell is that "morning-after" feeling—day after day after day.

Here on earth, feelings of guilt and shame can sometimes lead to good, such as greater self-control. In hell, however, no good comes of regret. Just more pain, more hardship, more desolation. Remembering will lead to self-accusation. Not only will people remember what they have done without the buffer of grace, but they will also remember what they rejected. They will remember friends, inviting them to church, and their refusing to come. They will remember being warned against destructive behaviors and how they scoffed. They will remember sitting impatiently in church saying, "Is he done yet? I gotta get home to watch the game!" They will remember their mother, saying to them, "I've prayed for you, child—when will you believe?" They will remember seeing their father on his knees, praying for them. They will remember receiving their Bible in Sunday school and then throwing it on the shelf to gather dust for the rest of their life. They will remember all the lost opportunities—and it will be hell.

IN HELL PEOPLE EXPERIENCE UNENDING RESTLESSNESS AND AFFLICTION

In addition to experiencing the full weight of sin and its consequences without the buffer of grace, those in hell will experience the unending misery of affliction. Again, this stands in stark contrast to heaven.

MISSING THE ETERNAL REST GOD OFFERS

Each time we consider a quality of hell, we need to remember the contrast with the qualities of heaven. One hallmark of heaven is the rest that God promises us. Hebrews 4:8-10 describes this: "This new place of rest was not the land of Canaan, where Joshua led them. If it had been, God would not have spoken later about another day of rest. So there is a special rest still waiting for the people of God. For all who enter into God's rest will find rest from their labors, just as God rested after creating the world" (NLT).

God created the heavens and the earth, and on the seventh day, he rested. Does that mean that God was exhausted? No! Heavenly rest is a far richer concept than simply the recovery of energy due to fatigue. God was not recovering his energy, for the Bible tells us he neither slumbers nor sleeps (Psalm 121:4). The "rest" of God is not marked by inertia, boredom, or fatigue. Heavenly rest is like the peace and joy that come from savoring the completion of a wonderful accomplishment. God was enjoying his creation. He was delighting in the work of his hands. Have you ever finished a project and felt absolutely invigorated by it? Perhaps you have that feeling when you look over your freshly mowed lawn or your newly weeded garden. Or maybe you feel that way when you repair an appliance or complete a hobby project. I have this feeling when I hold a published copy of one of my books. The work is completed, and the enjoyment begins.

Heavenly rest is like that feeling but even greater. In heaven we'll never be tired again:

We will rest from the weariness of the flesh.
We will rest from the temptations of the world,
the flesh, and the devil.
We will rest from the grief of life's heartaches and
longings.
We will rest from sorrow, anxiety, loneliness, and
confusion about God's will.
We will rest from guilt, failure, doubt, and
frustration.
We will rest from persecution, abuse, injustice,
and conflict.
We will rest from burdensome toil.
Hell will offer no such rest.

HELL IS A PLACE OF ENDLESS MISERY

Jesus conveys the nature of hell by using the term *Gehenna*. The term *Gehenna* describes the valley of Hinnom, west of Jerusalem, where at one time the Hebrews' children were sacrificed to the god Molech. Second Kings 16:2-3 tells that King Ahaz did not follow the ways of his ancestor David. Instead, he followed the example of the kings of Israel, even sacrificing his own son by fire. He imitated the detestable practices of the pagan nations that the Lord had driven from the land ahead of the Israelites. Ahaz offered sacrifices and burned incense at pagan shrines, on hills, and under every green tree. When good King Josiah rose to power, he desecrated the valley of Hinnom by making it a rubbish heap, a dump where all the refuse of Jerusalem was dumped and burned. It became a disgusting acreage of worms and maggots and smoldering fires. Images of hell as a place of undying worms and endless fires arise from this literal place outside Jerusalem.

There are a number of New Testament images for hell: It is described as a place of unquenchable and eternal fire (Mark 9:43), a place of outer darkness where there is weeping and gnashing of teeth (Matthew 25:30), a place where the undying worm torments hell's inhabitants (Mark 9:47-48). It is the lake of fire and brimstone (Revelation 20:10), the second death (Revelation 20:14). It is a place of destruction where the inhabitant is forever cut off from the presence of the Lord (2 Thessalonians 1:9).

The big question for a person today is, Are we supposed to take these literally? If you read Dante, the Italian poet of the Renaissance who produced a trilogy of books called *Paradise, Purgatory,* and *Inferno,* you find him describing these places literally. Dante describes hell as having rings, or regions, with different degrees of misery as punishment for different types of sin. The Bible is not so specific. We can't make a chart of hell from biblical material.

The nature of hell cannot be communicated in terms of landscapes and regions. It is about relationships. Whether you take the descriptions of hell literally or figuratively, this much I know: *These images point to a spiritual reality far more terrible than the means used to symbolize it or describe it.* How can a woman who's gone through labor describe that pain and anguish to a man who never will experience it? She may use a variety of images, but all will fall short of the mark. A family that has gone through wrenching grief cannot communicate the bitterness of their suffering to others who have never been touched by that kind of deep sorrow. How then can God communicate the horrors that await those who reject him? He takes the most excruciating experiences in life, the most destructive, disgusting, frightening forces of nature, and uses them as reference points. I personally believe there is a literal hell involving pain and misery at every level of being: physical, intellectual, emotional, relational, psychological, and spiritual. I don't fully understand the way it all works out, but I do know that I never want to find out!

The person who rejects Christ experiences the full weight of sin and its consequences—without the buffer of grace. He or she will also experience the unending misery of affliction in stark contrast to the rest that believers will have in heaven. But there's more. Having rejected the love God offers in Christ, those who go to hell will be cut off from love in all forms.

IN HELL PEOPLE EXPERIENCE ENDLESS
CONFLICT AND LONELINESS

If heaven is marked by love, hell is marred by hatred. There will be no home in hell. It is a place of wandering spirits who are never able to settle. Jesus alluded to this when he said, "When an evil spirit leaves a person, it goes into the desert, searching for rest. But when it finds none, it says, 'I will return to the person I came from.' So it returns and finds that its former home is all swept and clean. Then the spirit finds seven other spirits more evil than itself, and they all enter the person and live there. And so that person is worse off than before" (Luke 11:24-26, NLT).

Whereas heaven is a place of loving reconciliation, hell is a place of conflict. In Revelation 7, we are shown a heavenly gathering of all the tribes of the earth and people of all languages. They are reconciled and worshiping the Lord. (That's why it's so crucial for us to work for reconciliation on this earth—it is the model for life in heaven.) But in hell, it's each one for himself. The redemptive characteristics of the human spirit will be burned away in the fires of jealousy, antagonism, and ultimate self-centeredness.

The story is told of a scene from hell in which the occupants are seated at a marvelous banquet. The table is laden with exotic foods, each flawlessly presented. The aroma is intoxicating. But no one is eating. On closer examination, the observer sees that the people are fastened to their chairs, their arms fastened to splints prohibiting them from bending their elbows to feed themselves. Unable to reach the food, they are starving.

The scene then shifts to what appears to be the very same situation in heaven. The table is laden with the most exotic foods, each flawlessly presented. The aroma is intoxicating. The people are fastened to their chairs, their arms fastened to splints prohibiting them from bending their elbows to feed themselves. But the people are not starving. They are able to reach across the table and feed each other.

IF HELL IS SO BAD, WHAT KEEPS PEOPLE FROM CHOOSING HEAVEN?

The Bible makes it plain that those who choose life without God in this world must accept the results of that choice in the next. If you don't want God now, then you won't get him later.

But why wouldn't a person want heaven?

IGNORANCE

Many people have been led to believe the lie that if you lead a good life, you'll go to heaven. As we'll see in the next chapter, your definition of good is too low if you think your deeds will get you to heaven. Jesus Christ is the way, the truth, and the life.

UNBELIEF

There are people who say, "I just don't believe that stuff about heaven and hell." We've already seen how many people find it difficult to believe in heaven in our materialistic age. But some see that trend changing, as world-weary people are once again seeking out the spiritual side of life. For many, the question now becomes, Which heaven do you believe in? The heaven of human speculation or the one presented in biblical revelation? There is a huge gulf between them.

PRIDE

It's tough to admit that you may have been wrong. Feelings of embarrassment, shame, and foolishness churn in me when I've claimed to know something and am proven wrong. Pride is so strong that I'm sometimes tempted to ignore the truth. But pride can exact a heavy cost!

The gateway to hell is pride. The serpent in the garden lured Eve into sin with the prideful promise that she would be "like God." The temptations of Jesus in the wilderness were baited with pride and self-interest. The doorway to heaven, on the other hand, is humility. Humility acknowledges our proper place as creatures. Humility acknowledges that God is worthy of all honor. Humility confesses how we defied God and went our own way. Psalm 18:27 says, "You rescue those who are humble, but you humiliate the proud" (NLT). Psalm 147:6 says, "The Lord supports the humble, but he brings the wicked down into the dust," (NLT). Pride is the clenched fist that refuses all help. Humility is the open hand that receives God's grace.

PLEASURES AND SELF-INTEREST

So often we spend today at the expense of tomorrow. Pleasures of the moment can consume all our time and attention. We want to gratify our immediate needs and desires with little thought of the future. What will it take for us to learn that these pleasures never satisfy us fully? Why do we chase after the immediate, while ignoring the important?

The time comes for all of us when we realize the things of this earth cannot deliver the lasting joy and satisfaction for which we long. We are sated, but unsatisfied. The "Ecclesiastes syndrome" sets in as we cry out with the author, "I said to myself, 'Come now, I will make a test of pleasure; enjoy yourself.' But behold, this also was vanity. I said of laughter, 'It is mad,' and of pleasure, 'What use is it?'" (Ecclesiastes 2:1-2, RSV). Then we realize that we were made for more—much, much more.

NEGLECT

We're often just too busy to do anything about heaven. We think we'll get around to it later.

Some time ago I was asked to host a radio interview with several local pastors. I asked them to share their stories of how God had been changing lives in their congregations. Pastor Jeff told me about a man (let's call him Carl) who had initially come to church with his live-in fiancée. Carl's life was really a mess. A long-distance trucker, he often used drugs just to keep meeting his delivery schedules. At first, Carl wouldn't come into the church. He sat in the parking lot while his fiancée and his son by his first marriage went into the service. After several weeks Carl finally started coming in but stood by the back wall. He wouldn't take a seat.

One morning, Pastor Jeff felt constrained to give an altar call. "I'm not an 'altar call' kind of person," Pastor Jeff said in our radio interview. "I don't want to manipulate people with emotion and pressure, making them come down front. But God wouldn't let me go. And so finally I gave an altar call."

One of the first ones to come forward was Carl. Right behind him was his twelve-year-old son. Carl broke down and said, "I want a new life. I want to start over."

By God's grace Carl began to make a new start. He decided he had to quit the long-distance trucking business in order to break free from drugs and "loose living," to use his words. He found a local driving job, moved out of his fiancée's house, and made plans to marry her a few months later.

A few weeks after committing his life to Christ, Carl was out working in his driveway under his truck when the jacks collapsed. He was crushed to death instantly.

Pastor Jeff got a call from one of Carl's friends and went immediately to visit the family. What could he say to comfort them in such a tragedy?

"I confessed that I was extremely angry with God," said Jeff. "This man was just making a new start—and then this happens? It just didn't make sense."

But Carl's family was in a different place. The first

words spoken to the pastor were from Carl's son. "At least we know we're going to see him again!" he said.

"Can you imagine if this had happened to him and he didn't know Jesus Christ as Lord and Savior?" said his fiancée. "He's only been a believer for a few weeks, but now he is with Jesus!"

It's a good thing Carl didn't put off thinking about heaven.

THE TRUTH ABOUT CONSEQUENCES

There are consequences for the person who rejects God, who rejects God's revelation, who rejects God's salvation, who rejects God as Creator, and who rejects God as Redeemer. Such a person experiences these consequences in every aspect of his or her being and will experience them through all eternity—unless God intervenes.

We deserve hell. Through faith in Jesus Christ, God gives us heaven.

Hell is what a person earns. Heaven is what God gives.

The Puritan preacher Richard Baxter said, "If it were only for nothing and without our merit, the wonder of receiving heaven would be great. But it is moreover *against* our merit, and *against* our long endeavoring of our own ruin that God gives us heaven" (emphasis added).[3] Let me translate. That God would give us heaven simply as a gift is amazing—as amazing as if a person we barely knew handed us the keys to a multi-million-dollar mansion and property on the coast. We had never done anything special for him—why would he give us such a gift? But now imagine that same person, giving us the same gift *after* we had stolen his property, burned his house to the ground, and murdered his child. Unthinkable! Preposterous! Yet that is what God has done.

We've done things wrong, terribly wrong. We have defied God. We have misused his creation. We have ignored his love. And worst of all, we have been party to the murder, the crucifixion, of his Son. Yet God will give us heaven anyway, if we will simply receive his forgiveness through Christ.

By the grace of God, the only thing easier than going to hell is going to heaven. How do we get there? How can we be sure? That is the subject of the next chapter.

NOTES

1. *Northern California Christian Times,* 4, no. 6 (June 1998): 1. Copyright 1998, Visual Impressions, managing ed. Paul A. Hermann. Published under special licensing arrangements with KompuKeen Publishing, Inc., publishers of the *Southern California Christian Times.*

2. D. L. Moody, "Hell," in *20 Centuries of Great Preaching,* Clyde E. Fant Jr. and William M. Pinson Jr. (Waco: Word Books, 1971, VI), 314.

3. Richard Baxter, *The Saints' Everlasting Rest* (Grand Rapids: Baker Book House, 1978), 58.

CHAPTER SIX

"How Can I Be Sure I'll Go to Heaven?"

Remember Ann, the woman with cancer whose story I told in the first chapter? She's the one who, when I first visited her, said, "I'm not sure I believe in heaven and hell and Jesus and the Bible and all that stuff. But if you still want to talk, come on in." Ann was a blunt, to-the-point kind of person! I want to tell you the rest of her story. Over the weeks and months that I visited with Ann, we discussed her doubts and objections to the Christian faith. At the point when she knew death was coming, Ann said she wanted to know if she could have eternal life. "I really want to make contact with God and live with him forever. If all this turns out to be false," she said with typical candor, "I won't have lost anything. But if it's true," she said, then paused, "I *really* want it."

Ann faced the questions we *all* will face one day: What lies beyond the grave? Is there eternal life? If so, how can I be certain I will go to heaven? Is there any way to know for sure? I shared a series of biblical passages and principles with Ann that I have shared with hundreds of people in various ways. I'm going to walk through them now as I did with Ann.

STOP TRUSTING YOURSELF

When I first asked Ann if she thought she would go to heaven, she said, "Well, I hope so. I've tried to lead a good life." This is the most common response people give—but, as I gently told Ann, it's based on a misunderstanding of God's plan.

The fact is that no one is good enough to earn heaven. We usually assess our life by comparison with others. We think that because we haven't robbed a bank, murdered someone, or committed gross immorality, we are in good standing with God. What we fail to realize is that God's standard is perfection—and all of us have fallen short. Romans 3:23 says, "For all have sinned; all fall short of God's glorious standard" (NLT).

There are different standards of goodness. We may say that a dog is good because it is housebroken and doesn't bite. But the standard of goodness for a child is much higher. God's standard for people is communicated in the Ten Commandments (see Exodus 20) and is clarified by Jesus' Sermon on the Mount. Jesus makes it clear that anger is as liable to judgment as murder, and that lust is as much of a violation as adultery (Matthew 5:21-30).

Sin is not a popular word in our day. Neither is cancer. Nevertheless, we must deal with both of them because they are both killers. One of the great mistakes we make with regard to sin is measuring ourselves by comparison with others instead of by God's standard. Compared to others, we may be relatively good. But compared to God's standards, it's a far different story.

A man came in to talk with me after I performed his mother's funeral. He had attended church as a child but stopped when he became a teenager. He was questioning the assertion that we all have sinned. Because of his background in law, I asked him what it took to convict a person of a crime. "The evidence has to prove a person guilty beyond a reasonable doubt," he replied.

I read him the Ten Commandments and Jesus' comments on them in Matthew 5. "If you were a prosecutor operating on the basis of Jesus' definition of murder, do you think there is anyone who is innocent beyond a reasonable doubt?"

He smiled and shook his head. "If that's the Lord's standard—we don't stand a chance!"

The answer to the question of what's good enough all depends on the standard. I've heard the example of a person making a three-egg omelet. Let's say you are making the omelet and you crack the first two eggs and drop them in a bowl. But then the third egg turns out to be rotten. Would you go ahead and make the omelet with the bad egg? No, because the one rotten egg would contaminate the two good ones. The bad one ruins the whole thing.

Imagine that you've constructed a hot-air balloon made of patches sewn together. Now, you remove a tiny patch. It isn't very big, but it leaves a hole. Would you go up in that balloon? Would you risk your life on it? Of course not. One little hole would make the entire balloon collapse. "And the person who keeps all of the laws except one is as guilty as the person who has broken all of God's laws" (James 2:10, NLT). We fall short of the Lord's standard and into judgment.

Why is it important to understand this? Because if we think we must trust in ourselves, we'll be wrong—dead wrong.

START TRUSTING JESUS CHRIST

When I was in ninth grade, I attended a special service at our church that changed my whole life. I didn't really care much for going to church in those days. Few students from my school attended our church, and I didn't feel as though I belonged. I believed in God, but my knowledge was limited, and my faith made little difference in my daily life. Then I heard a message that changed everything. The preacher compared the human situation to standing at the edge of the Grand Canyon. God is on one side of the chasm, and we are on the other. The chasm that separates us from God was formed by our sin. So we are cut off. We are helpless to reach God on our own. No matter how rich we are, no matter how powerful, no matter how smart, no matter how popular, no matter how athletic, we cannot possibly jump across the mile-wide gap! If we tried, we would plunge straight to the bottom.

The only way across the chasm would be to find a bridge. And, the preacher went on to explain, Christ is the bridge to God. He came to earth to die in our place.

His cross forms the connecting link by which we may come back to God. I have since learned that this is a common analogy for faith, but for me it was new information. Even at that age, I was able to understand how much I needed Jesus Christ. I knew I couldn't connect to God on my own.

Jesus entered this world to open the way for us to enter heaven. He came to identify with us. Even though he is the Son of God, he did not remain aloof but entered fully into human life. The Bible describes what he did in this way:

> Because God's children are human beings—made of flesh and blood—Jesus also became flesh and blood by being born in human form. For only as a human being could he die, and only by dying could he break the power of the Devil, who had the power of death. Only in this way could he deliver those who have lived all their lives as slaves to the fear of dying.
>
> We all know that Jesus came to help the descendants of Abraham, not to help the angels. Therefore, it was necessary for Jesus to be in every respect like us, his brothers and sisters, so that he could be our merciful and faithful High Priest before God. He then could offer a sacrifice that would take away the sins of the people. Since he himself has gone through suffering and temptation, he is able to help us when we are being tempted. (Hebrews 2:14-18, NLT)

If you've ever worked for somebody else, you know the difference between a boss who stands apart and one who "gets his or her hands dirty." At a senior-high summer camp, the students on the kitchen work crew were staying away from the grease pit. That's understandable: It was a gooey mess after being filled daily with the grease from cooking bacon, sausage, hamburgers, and other goodies for over five hundred campers. Finally, the work-crew boss showed up. "Hey, gang! Wanna have some fun?" he called out. "Here's how it's done." With that, he took off his socks and shoes, rolled up his pants, stepped into the grease, and started shoveling it out. What could the others do? Off came their shoes and socks, up went their pant legs, and in they went. In seconds, laughter filled the area, and a crowd gathered. Believe it or not, others wanted to get in there with them. All because the boss got dirty first.

Jesus entered the mess of our life. He experienced poverty, rejection, misunderstanding, pressure, stress, exhaustion, the gooey grease pit of our life—and cleaned it all!

A number of years ago, I heard a story attributed to Ernest Gordon, a World War II soldier who became a prisoner of war of the Japanese. His story is told in the book *Through the Valley of the Kwai*. As recounted in the book, a group of soldiers was captured by the Japanese. Each day they had to go down into the mire and the muck of a river, with minimal food, in the wretched heat of the tropics, to dig the footings for a bridge. When they returned to the prison camp at the end of each day, the soldiers would count the shovels while the prisoners were lined up. Only after the shovels were inventoried would the prisoners get a little bit of rice and a little bit of water.

One day when the soldiers brought the prisoners back and counted the tools, they discovered that one shovel was missing. The soldiers wouldn't permit anyone to leave the inspection area until the thief confessed. Nobody moved. The soldiers threatened them with severe punishment and loss of their daily food rations unless someone confessed or "ratted." Still nobody moved. The tension was electrifying. Then one prisoner stood forward. The other prisoners were stunned. This was the last man they would have suspected. He was a well-respected follower of Christ in that camp who had prayed and encouraged them with Bible verses when they had no hope. How could he have done this? As the other prisoners watched in horror, the Japanese guards took their guns and shovels and beat the man to death. They then dismissed the other prisoners. Afterwards, two of the guards went back into the work room and counted the shovels. They were all there. Not a single shovel was missing! The guards had miscounted. An innocent prisoner had died so the others wouldn't have to.

Hearing this story, we are indignant. We say, "That's so unfair!" One innocent man dying so that others could be saved—that *is* unfair! But it's just what the Lord did for us. He took our place. That's substitution. And with God there's no miscounting. We are justly accused and truly guilty. That's what we mean when we say believe in God. What do we believe in? We believe that we deserve judgment. But we also believe that Jesus took our place. He was beaten and killed so we wouldn't have to be.

Some of us try to be saved through our own efforts. In my book *SoulShaping*, I call it the mathematics of salvation.[1] We try to *add* good works to our life to impress God. Or we *subtract* things, like watching TV or playing golf on Sunday, trying to curry God's favor. Or we *multiply* our activities, being busy for God, as if he were looking for spiritual workaholics. Or we *divide* our life so that we have a "sacred compartment" where we attend church regularly or give donations that acknowledge our duty toward the Lord. But none of these "add up" to salvation.

Here's God's arithmetic: *Christ plus nothing equals everything.* The basis of our salvation is what God has done for us by sending Jesus Christ to die for us. Jesus clearly communicated this to his disciples as he was facing crucifixion:

> "Don't be troubled. You trust God, now trust in me. There are many rooms in my Father's home, and I am going to prepare a place for you. If this were not so, I would tell you plainly. When everything is ready, I will come and get you, so that you will always be with me where I am. And you know where I am going and how to get there."
>
> "No, we don't know, Lord," Thomas said. "We haven't any idea where you are going, so how can we know the way?"

Jesus told him, "I am the way, the truth, and the life. No one can come to the Father except through me. If you had known who I am, then you would have known who my Father is. From now on you know him and have seen him!" (John 14:1-7, NLT)

Our comfort and security are founded on what Jesus does, not on what we do.

Don't be troubled—trust Jesus.
Don't be anxious—Jesus has prepared a place for us.
Don't be afraid—Jesus will come again and take us home.
Don't trust in anyone or anything else—Jesus alone is the way, the truth, and the life.

What happens when you believe in Jesus? You will receive this promise: God has a place for you. Jesus builds it, Jesus furnishes it, Jesus takes you there, and Jesus hands you the keys. That's the way of the gospel. He stood in our place so that we could be in his—forever.

This promise is ours through faith. In Romans 1:17, we read, "For in the gospel a righteousness from God is revealed, a righteousness that is by faith from first to last, just as it is written: 'The righteous will live by faith'" (NIV). But what is faith? Is it just wishful thinking—or something more?

To answer that question, I want to tell you the story that I told Ann some years ago. Many have heard the story since. But it is worth repeating because it is one of the most vivid demonstrations of faith you'll ever hear. The story is told of a French tightrope walker in the 1800s named Blondin. Blondin decided he wanted to walk a tightrope over Niagara Falls. His first challenge was in stringing a cable across the falls. To accomplish this, Blondin and his manager gave kites to a number of children. They attached strands of wire to the kites and flew them from the American shore to the Canadian shore, where workers would wind them into the high-wire cable. The cable was then strung from one-hundred-foot towers right above the thundering brink of the falls. As Blondin climbed the tower and stood on the platform, the crowd watched in anxious anticipation. "How many of you think I can walk across this tightrope?" Blondin shouted. The crowd applauded, and Blondin started out onto the cable. The only sound that could be heard was the roar of the falls as Blondin crossed to one side and back again. Astounding! Then the great performer challenged the crowd, "How many of you think I can carry a person across?" The crowd went wild with excitement. Then he dared them, "Volunteers?" The crowd fell silent.

Can you imagine the feeling that swept through the people at that moment? It's one thing to watch someone else take a risk. But to put your own life on the line—that's something different!

Not surprisingly, there were no volunteers from the crowd. But, having had no prior discussion, Blondin was surprised to see his manager climbing up the tower. He got onto Blondin's shoulders, and Blondin began walking across the tightrope. About halfway across, several of the wires in the cable snapped. The cable jolted, and the crowd gasped. The manager cried out, "What do we do?"

"Become one with me," said Blondin. "However I move, you move. Whatever I do, you do. And we both will live." And they did.

I told that story to Ann. When I had finished I asked her quietly, "So, Ann, do you want to get on Jesus' shoulders now? You're about to cross a raging cataract of death. But you'll make it if you go with Jesus."

"Yes," she said. "I want to get on his shoulders. I'm ready. I feel like I don't have to climb a staircase to God anymore. I feel like he's right here with me."

"Ann, remember when you got married? You had to stand in front of a pastor and in front of witnesses in order to express your commitment to Don. That's what you need to do now. Tell Jesus you love him, and make your promises to him."

I invited Ann to pray. Over the years, I have led people to Christ in a number of ways. Sometimes I pray, and they repeat what I say. Sometimes I just sit with people as they pray in silence and then say "amen" aloud when they are finished. When I invited Ann to pray, she said she wanted to pray out loud. This was her prayer: "Dear God, dear, dear, Lord Jesus. Thank you for being so patient with me. I've always wanted to believe, but I just didn't understand. I'm getting on your shoulders now. I believe in you. Wash away all my sin. I'm so very sorry. Now carry me and forgive me when I get scared. This is really hard, Lord, but you are making it so much easier. And Lord, watch over Don. Help him to get on your shoulders too. In Jesus' name, amen."

When I looked up at Ann, I saw a health and joy in her face like I had never seen there before.

"I'm going to see him soon," she whispered.

A few days later, several church leaders and I gathered in Ann's living room, where a hospital bed had been set up. And there in her bed, I baptized her. Then we shared the Lord's Supper. Afterward, her husband, Don, who had loved her, nursed her, and watched her battle an awful disease, said, "I feel like it's our wedding day."

Two months later, Ann got on Jesus' shoulders and walked across that thundering chasm to the Other Side. I know the crowds of heaven were cheering. Ann had been so peaceful in her final weeks and days. When I went into her hospital room just minutes after her death, I could see the peace lingering on her sweet face.

BE CONFIDENT OF YOUR HEAVENLY HOPE

Once we understand the judgment we deserve because of our sinful rebellion, we are awed by God's grace in welcoming us into heaven through Christ. But what if you're still struggling with doubt? What if you're still not sure there's a place for you in heaven?

It's almost impossible not to be moved by the Vietnam War Memorial in Washington, D.C. The V-shaped wall of polished black granite is etched with more than fifty-eight thousand individual names of United States soldiers who died or were declared missing in action in that terrible conflict. As people find their friends' names, it's common to see them making rubbings on paper, tears filling their eyes. How much more moving will it be when the Book of Life is opened—and there we will read not of those lost in conflict but of those won back from death! There will be tears and shouts of joy, exclamations of gratitude and praise.

God's Word gives a number of promises forming a solid foundation for our assurance of salvation. In John's Gospel, Jesus says, "My sheep recognize my voice; I know them, and they follow me. I give them eternal life, and they will never perish. No one will snatch them away from me, for my Father has given them to me, and he is more powerful than anyone else. So no one can take them from me. The Father and I are one" (John 10:27-30, NLT).

God is able to hold on to us. Nothing in this life or beyond this life can separate us from the Lord:

> Since God did not spare even his own Son but gave him up for us all, won't God, who gave us Christ, also give us everything else?
>
> Who dares accuse us whom God has chosen for his own? Will God? No! He is the one who has given us right standing with himself. Who then will condemn us? Will Christ Jesus? No, for he is the one who died for us and was raised to life for us and is sitting at the place of highest honor next to God, pleading for us.
>
> Can anything ever separate us from Christ's love? Does it mean he no longer loves us if we have trouble or calamity, or are persecuted, or

are hungry or cold or in danger or threatened with death? (Even the Scriptures say, "For your sake we are killed every day; we are being slaughtered like sheep.") No, despite all these things, overwhelming victory is ours through Christ, who loved us.

And I am convinced that nothing can ever separate us from his love. Death can't, and life can't. The angels can't, and the demons can't. Our fears for today, our worries about tomorrow, and even the powers of hell can't keep God's love away. Whether we are high above the sky or in the deepest ocean, nothing in all creation will ever be able to separate us from the love of God that is revealed in Christ Jesus our Lord. (Romans 8:32-39, NLT)

God will complete the work he has begun in us. "And I am sure that God, who began the good work within you, will continue his work until it is finally finished on that day when Christ Jesus comes back again" (Philippians 1:6, NLT).

The apostle Paul displays a confidence that should mark all of us when he writes, "The time of my death is near. I have fought a good fight, I have finished the race, and I have remained faithful. And now the prize awaits me—the crown of righteousness that the Lord, the righteous Judge, will give me on that great day of his return. And the prize is not just for me but for all who eagerly look forward to his glorious return" (2 Timothy 4:6-8, NLT).

How can you know for sure that you're going to heaven? You can trust God to keep his word. God's promise isn't a license for carelessness but an assurance of comfort and confidence. You don't have to wait until you die to find out your final destination. You don't have to doubt. You shouldn't put this book down without knowing for sure you're going to heaven. You simply have to answer this question: Are you on Christ's shoulders? If you can say yes, then he will carry you all the way there.

Let me close this chapter with a prayer you can make your own:

> Oh, Lord, our God, thank you for Jesus Christ. Thank you for removing my blindness to the truth about Jesus Christ and the eternal hope that I can have through him. Lord, I believe in you. I confess my sin and put my full trust in you. I want to be sure I will go to heaven, so I'm getting on your shoulders now. I pray that I'll not only trust you as my Savior but also obey you as my Lord and Master. I want your word to be my word and your action to be my action. I ask this in Jesus' name, amen.

NOTES

1. Douglas J. Rumford, *SoulShaping* (Wheaton, Ill.: Tyndale House Publishers, Inc., 1996), 38–51.

CHAPTER SEVEN

"What Difference Does Heaven Make Today?"

Have you ever heard somebody described as "so heavenly minded, he's no earthly good"? There are those who think so much about the next life that they contribute nothing in this life. For these folks, thinking about heaven becomes an escape from reality. The prospect of eternal life becomes an excuse for avoiding responsibilities in this present life. Heaven has little positive impact on their daily life and may even have a negative impact.

Others simply avoid the thought of heaven altogether. Someone once said, "Young people don't want to think about heaven because it's too far away, and old folks don't want to think about it because it's getting too close." For these "avoiders," thinking of heaven is either irrelevant or morbid. They live in a state of denial, like the student who never goes to class but somehow expects to pass.

So what good does it do to think about heaven? Is

there a healthy way to think about the *next* life that brings benefits to *this* life?

The plain teaching of God's Word is that our heavenly hope is not only a comfort for the future but a catalyst for the present. A full understanding of heaven empowers a joyful, responsible life now. In other words, *the way you think about heaven can totally change how you live your life on this earth.*

C. S. Lewis, in his book *Mere Christianity,* talks about hope and about heaven:

> It does not mean that we are to leave the present world as it is. If you read history you will find that the Christians who did most for the present world were just those who thought most of the next. The Apostles themselves, who set on foot the conversion of the Roman Empire, the great men who built up the Middle Ages, the English Evangelicals who abolished the Slave Trade, all left their mark on Earth, precisely because their minds were occupied with Heaven. It is since Christians have largely ceased to think of the other world that they have become so ineffective in this. Aim at Heaven and you will get earth "thrown in": aim at earth and you will get neither.[1]

The prospect of a future life in heaven makes a difference in literally every aspect of life. In this chapter we're going to survey seven principles for living with a heavenly mind-set.

FOCUS DAILY ON THINGS THAT ARE ABOVE

One of the secrets of a satisfying life is keeping your ultimate goal in mind. Steven Covey, author of *The 7 Habits of Highly Effective People* and *First Things First,* highlights the principle he calls "begin with the end in mind." He writes, "How different our lives are when we really know what is deeply important to us, and, keeping that picture in mind, we manage ourselves each day to be and to do what really matters most."[2] When we lose sight of the goal, we get caught up in petty distractions.

I would like to take this concept a step further and talk about "The End," meaning the end of our life. In Colossians 3:1-2 Paul writes, "Since, then, you have been raised with Christ [note the *past* tense—speaking the resurrection reality that is ours *now*], set your hearts on things above, where Christ is seated at the right hand of God. Set your minds on things above, not on earthly things." Verse 1 exhorts us to set our *heart* on things that are above, and verse 2 focuses on our *mind.* We are to set our whole being—heart and mind—on things above.

A friend of mine named Jean is someone who sets her whole being on things above. Jean has spent most of the last twenty years in a wheelchair. She was adopted as a child; the only thing she knows about her birth parents is that they didn't want her. She's battled cancer and numerous physical ailments. But if you met her, all you'd remember would be her smile. When I encounter someone like Jean who has struggled throughout life, I often ask the question, "How do you keep your joy?" Jean's answer has stayed with me for years, "Doug, I learned long ago that this world never keeps it promises. So I don't expect much from life. But I know—I mean *I know!*—that I will be with the Lord in heaven. So I tell him every day, 'Lord, until I am with you, I will live for you.' You'd be amazed how that helps."

Lord, until I am with you, I will live for you. Now *that* is living with "The End" in mind.

When the prospect of heaven is foremost in our mind each day, we live differently. We don't focus on what we are missing in this life but on what is awaiting us in the next. The assurance of heaven as our final destination gives us perspective. When our mind and heart are set on heaven, we are not devastated by disappointments in this world. We are not controlled by worldly priorities. We are not compelled to impress others or to be intimidated by them. When we're aiming for heaven, we're free to focus on what is pleasing to God, on his higher purposes for our life.

HOLD EARTHLY THINGS LOOSELY

We get anxious and frustrated because we hold too tightly to worldly things—social position in the community, prestigious titles, possessions. Jesus reminded us that the things of this world never last or give lasting satisfaction: "Do not store up for yourselves treasures on earth, where moth and rust destroy, and where thieves break in and steal. But store up for yourselves treasures in heaven, where moth and rust do not destroy, and where thieves do not break in and steal. For where your treasure is, there your heart will be also" (Matthew 6:19).

A HEAVENLY MIND IS NOT PREOCCUPIED
WITH THINGS OF EARTH

When we focus on heaven, we look differently at all the material attractions and activities of this world. On the other hand, when we tighten our grip on life, God may allow harsh circumstances to loosen it. E. M. Bounds writes, "Great earthly attachments lessen heavenly attachments. The heart which indulges itself in great earthly loves, will have less love for heaven. God's great work and often His most afflictive and chastening work is to unfasten our hearts from earth, and fasten them to heaven, to break up and desolate the earthly home, so that we may seek a home in heaven."[3]

When my wife and I bought our first new car, I spent a lot more time than normal cleaning, polishing, and just admiring it. Then, within a week, the bumper got dented—and I got depressed! After a day or so, I suddenly realized that I was giving too much emotional energy to a material object. The heavenly mind may appreciate an automobile but doesn't get preoccupied with it.

A WORLDLY MIND SEES THIS LIFE
AS AN END IN ITSELF

Some people spend their whole life in a race for money, power, prestige, and recognition. They want others to remember them when they're gone, maybe put up a monument to them. Jeremy Taylor wrote, "Many people, by great labors and affronts, many indignities and crimes, labor only for a pompous epitaph and loud title upon their marble."[4]

What good will it be *to you* if somebody says something

good about you after you die? You're not going to hear it. And what good is a monument *to you* when you're gone? A "loud title upon marble" will not impress the Lord God Almighty, who will ask you what you did with the gifts he gave you and how you honored his name and how you loved your neighbor as yourself. What greater tragedy could there be than to labor your whole life, accumulating the treasures and experiences of this earth—only to find that they do you no lasting good. The only thing that will do you any good is to realize that you will have eternal life through Jesus Christ.

A HEAVENLY MIND SEES EVERYTHING IN THIS LIFE AS A MEANS TO "THE END"

The heavenly mind looks for the call of God in the dailiness of life. A fast-food cashier, a custodian, a journalist, a medical technician, or a homemaker—in short, *anyone in any job* can find a means of caring for people as Jesus would, of providing practical service in a godly way. If you spend your days thinking about what you need to do in order to advance, you may very well miss the call of God, because God's call is often rooted in sacrifice.

Jesus taught us to store up treasures in heaven by means of our earthly goods. "One thing you lack," he said [to a rich young ruler]. "Go, sell everything you have and give to the poor, and you will have treasure in heaven. Then come, follow me" (Mark 10:21).

All of life, not just money, is a means by which we can develop and demonstrate our faith and faithfulness. The way we exercise stewardship of all our responsibilities in this life has eternal implications. Jesus taught this in the story of the master who left his servants in charge of his estate and then returned for an accounting—a time of judgment. To the faithful servants he said:

> Well done, good and faithful servant! You have been faithful with a few things; I will put you in charge of many things. Come and share your master's happiness! (Matthew 25:21, 23)

But to the unfaithful servant he said:

> You wicked, lazy servant! So you knew that I harvest where I have not sown and gather where I have not scattered seed? Well then, you should have put my money on deposit with the bankers, so that when I returned I would have received it back with interest.
>
> Take the talent from him and give it to the one who has the ten talents. For everyone who has will be given more, and he will have an abundance. Whoever does not have, even what he has will be taken from him. And throw that worthless servant outside, into the darkness, where there will be weeping and gnashing of teeth. (Matthew 25:26-30)

What we do in this life prepares us for the next.

ENDURE SUFFERING COURAGEOUSLY

William Booth, the founder of the Salvation Army, was having serious eye trouble. He was experiencing episodes when the most he could see was the shapes of objects. Although his condition was getting worse and worse, he held out hope that it would be reversed. Then one day his son, Bramwell, came to give his father the word that there would be no recovery.

"Do you mean that I'm always going to be blind?" Booth asked.

"I fear that is what we must contemplate, Father," his son said.

"You mean, I'll never see your face again?"

"No, Father, probably not in this world."

"Bramwell," said Booth, "I've done what I could for God and for people with my eyes; now I'm going to do what I can for God and for people without my eyes." And with that he went on.[5]

The apostle Paul writes, "I consider that our present sufferings are not worth comparing with the glory that will be revealed in us" (Romans 8:18). Suffering is a part of life in this fallen world. There are no guarantees that we're going to have life, liberty, and happiness, no matter what the world says. In fact, at the heart of our faith is the Cross, the sign of the most excruciating suffering that was ever endured.

Playwright Arthur Miller once wrote of the agony of writing: "Controlled hysteria is what's required," Miller said. "To exist constantly in a state of controlled hysteria. It's agony. But everyone has agony. The difference is that I try to take my agony home and teach it to sing."[6]

Because William Booth had the hope of heaven, he made his agony a song of courage and inspiration. He conveyed no bitterness at the prospect of blindness. He showed no resentment. He faced the difficulties of life with eager confidence that God was sending him on a new adventure. When we are heavenly minded, as William Booth was, we endure suffering courageously.

The hope of heaven stimulates not only courage in the face of danger but tenacity in the face of persecution. Pastor and theologian Martin Niemöller defied Hitler and spent many months in a German concentration camp preceding and during World War II. When he was first captured, his father, Pastor Heinrich Niemöller, received a visit from the pastor of an American church in Berlin, Dr. Turner. During the visit Pastor Niemöller exhorted Dr. Turner, "When you go back to America, do not let anyone pity the father and mother of Martin Niemöller. Only pity any follower of Christ who does not know the joy that is set before those who endure the cross, despising the shame. Yes, it is a horrible thing to have a son in a concentration camp. But there would be something more terrible for us: if God had needed a faithful martyr and our Martin had been unwilling."[7]

Persecution is a terrible thing, but unfaithfulness is far worse. The hope of heaven gives us the ability to stay faithful in the face of persecution.

SERVE GOD FAITHFULLY

Several years into my pastoral ministry I began to keep a journal about my struggles with serving. The realities of ministry weren't fulfilling my expectations. I wrote the following, which I now call "A Servant Protests":

I remember saying to the Lord, "OK, Lord, I'll serve you." But I expected to work on my own terms. *When I protested the long hours,* the Lord said, "But I heard you say you'd be my *servant.* Time is my gift to you. I promise you an eternity of joy."

When I asked for pleasures to amuse me, the Lord smiled, "But I heard you say you'd be my *servant.* The pleasures that I have for you are beyond comparison. But you're looking in the wrong place for them."

When I asked him to remove the pain, the Lord said, "But I heard you say you'd be my *servant.* My service is to the human heart—a place of pain. You will feel the pain of those who are broken. That is the only way I can heal."

When I cried because I felt so alone, the Lord said, "Alone? You are never alone. But if you're wrapped up in yourself, you miss me. I am with you. You don't seem to take that very seriously. Believe! I am with you always. And I have given you my children, too. You'll find they're a lot like you."

In the silence of the moment, I realized that the Master of the Universe was not a tyrant but my father. His only Son had rolled up his sleeves to sweat and serve among us. This Jesus—a servant to whom no nobility can compare.

"OK, Lord," I said. "I really do want to be your servant. It won't be easy. And I'll probably start grumbling again. I'm not even sure I have the stuff it takes. But, if you'll have me, I'm yours."

"I want you—now and forever," he said.

As I reread this journal entry, I am reminded of how central is the hope of eternal life. We are *not* to live for the immediate rewards of this life, *not* for what this world has to offer. We are asked to sacrifice now for the joy that will one day be ours with Christ. We are asked to pay the price now for the timeless investment it secures.

Some of us are easily discouraged with this world. There are times when it seems like it's just too far gone. I confess that sometimes I want to give up. I am tempted to say, "God, I've done what I could, and it's done no good. So forget it. I'm sick of being disappointed, I'm sick of being let down, and I'm sick of being in the minority. I'm sick of being the only one who will speak up in a certain situation. I am done!"

When I'm feeling this way, it helps to remember what 1 Corinthians 15:58 says: "Therefore, my dear brothers, stand firm. Let nothing move you. Always give yourself fully to the work of the Lord, because you know that your labor in the Lord is not in vain."

The Lord says, "Serve me. It's not in vain. Give yourself fully to my work. It's not in vain."

I may protest, "But God, people aren't listening to your Word."

And the Lord replies, "What did my Son do?"

"But God," I continue, "They're not changing. They're not doing things any differently!"

And the Lord simply says, "What did my Son do?"

Give yourself fully to the work of the Lord. It will not be in vain. Perhaps you've been tempted to give up on church. Maybe you've been tempted to give up on witnessing for Christ. Or to give up on praying for some of your neighbors or your family members. To give up on your marriage. To give up on your kids. But the word of the Lord to you is "Serve faithfully." It's not in vain.

We serve faithfully because, by serving, we glorify God. It pleases God when we use our gifts, no matter what the results are. Likewise, by serving we touch the lives of people who need to know the Lord. They can't always understand our profession of faith, but they can understand our service. So we join with the Lord that his kingdom may come and his will be done on earth as it is in heaven.

RESIST TEMPTATION DILIGENTLY

Moments of temptation may become either thorns of accusation or crowns of victory, depending on how we respond. Second Corinthians 5:10 gives us this sobering reminder: "We must all appear before the judgment seat of Christ, that each one may receive what is due him for the things done while in the body, whether good or bad."

Judgment Day is coming.

It's tempting to rationalize sin with the thought, "It doesn't really matter because God will forgive me anyway." Oh, yes, God will forgive you, but it may be at a cost that you would never want to pay. There may consequences that will carry forward throughout your life.

The story of David's sin with Bathsheba is the most vivid biblical example of the principle that forgiveness removes the eternal punishment for sin, but it may not remove the human consequences (see another book in this series, *What about Unanswered Prayer?*, where I devote an entire chapter to exploring this principle). The prophet Nathan delivered to David the news of the long-term consequences of his sin:

> Why have you despised the word of the Lord,
> to do what is evil in his sight? You have smitten
> Uriah the Hittite with the sword, and have taken
> his wife to be your wife, and have slain him with
> the sword of the Ammonites. Now therefore
> the sword shall never depart from your house,
> because you have despised me, and have taken
> the wife of Uriah the Hittite to be your wife.
> (2 Samuel 12:9-10, RSV)

David experienced family conflict throughout the rest of his life. This situation serves as a warning against the abuse of grace. Sin says, "It's just a small thing. Who's going to know?" The Bible says one day everyone will know: "Everything that is now hidden or secret will eventually be brought to light" (Mark 4:22, NLT). Someday we will answer to the Lord for all our behavior.

When we are living for heaven, when we have the perspective of eternity, we resist temptation diligently. We resist it because we know what it cost Jesus to secure our forgiveness. We resist it because we know that sin has eternal consequences. We long to live so that when we look back, there will be no shame and no regret. That doesn't mean that we will never sin. It means that we will strengthen ourselves against temptations by considering the eternal cost and our ultimate accountability to God. We will follow the example of saints of old, who often quenched the sparks of temptation by asking themselves, "How will I look back on this moment from my deathbed?"

WITNESS CONSISTENTLY TO YOUR HEAVENLY HOPE

We all need hope—but it must be a hope rooted in reality. Sadly, the messages our culture hears about the future tend to be based on three lies.

First, there is the lie that everybody is going to heaven, no matter what.

Second, there is the lie that there's no future beyond this life. That there's no heaven or hell. That this world is all there is. That you should therefore go for all you can get now, no matter what you do to anybody along the way.

Third, there's the lie that hope is all up to you. Make your own meaning. Create your own religion. Find your own spirituality. Do your own good works, and God will be impressed with you.

These are lies of false hope, no hope, and self-created hope. People need to hear the genuine message of Christian, heavenly hope—that in Jesus Christ, God has done for us what we could never do for ourselves.

When we are living for heaven, we witness to our heavenly hope. In 1 Peter 3:15, Peter exhorts us to speak boldly about our hope: "In your hearts set apart Christ as Lord. Always be prepared to give an answer to everyone who asks you to give the reason for the hope that you have. But do this with gentleness and respect."

Do people look at you and say, "Why are you so hopeful?" I confess that too often I'm not as joyful and hopeful as I wish I were. But hope grows as we think about our heavenly destiny. Hope grows as we meditate on God's promise of eternal life and the joy that will one day be ours. "No eye has seen, no ear has heard, no mind has conceived what God has prepared for those who love him" (1 Corinthians 2:9).

FACE DEATH CONFIDENTLY

Death is the most fearful enemy we ever will face, and it is closer than we may realize—as I was reminded one day during a road trip with three church members. We were driving early one morning to Bakersfield, California, two hours south of Fresno, traveling down Highway 99, the main road through the central valley. As often happens in the winter months, a thick fog blanketed the area. We arrived safely, but returning home in the midafternoon, we saw the remnants of a seventy-plus car pileup in which two people had been killed and a number of others injured. It was the worst accident of its kind in California history. The tragedy occurred just ninety minutes after we had driven through the same area. Five or six hours later, workmen were still trying to clear the tangled mess of trucks and cars. We had escaped by a matter of minutes.

Death could come at any time, but because we are living for heaven, we can face it confidently. As he lay dying, Puritan preacher Richard Baxter is reported to have said, "I have pain; but I have peace. I have peace." This is just one of countless testimonies to the promise of I Corinthians 15:54: "Death has been swallowed up in victory." In another such testimony, G. W. Ridout reports the dying moments of D. L. Moody:

> Awakening from a sleep, he [Moody] said,
> "Earth recedes. Heaven opens before me. If this
> is death, it is sweet! There is no valley here. God
> is calling me and I must go." His son, who was
> standing by his bedside said, "No, no, father,
> you are dreaming."
>
> "No," said Mr. Moody, "I am not dreaming:
> I have been within the gates: I have seen the
> children's faces." A short time elapsed and
> then, following what seemed to the family to
> be the death struggle, he spoke again: "This
> is my triumph: This is my coronation day! It
> is glorious!"[8]

Because we are living for heaven, we can banish the fear of death. It does not have the final say. Writing in the 1600s, pastor Jeremy Taylor observed that, for those who have placed their faith in Christ, death can be a haven.

God having in this world placed us in a sea, and troubled the sea with a continual storm, hath appointed the church for a ship, and religion to be the stern; but there is no haven nor port but death. Death is that harbor whither God hath designed every one, that there he may find rest from the troubles of the world. Either therefore let us be willing to die when God calls, or let us never more complain of the calamities of our life which we feel so sharp and numerous. And when God sends His angel to us with the scroll of death, let us look on it as an act of mercy, to prevent many sins and many calamities of a longer life, and lay our heads down softly, and go to sleep without wrangling like babies and froward children. For a man at least gets this by death, that his calamities are not immortal.[9]

Sam Shoemaker had such an outlook on life. An Episcopal priest, he played a major role in initiating the present-day small-group movement. He was also instrumental in founding Alcoholics Anonymous, especially in developing AA's twelve steps. Near the end of his life he wrote:

As I sit in the study on a beautiful, cool August afternoon, I look back with many thanks. It has been a great run. I wouldn't have missed it for anything. Much could and should have been better and I have by no means done what I should have done with all that I've been given, but the overall experience of being alive has been thrilling. I believe that death is a doorway to more of it: clearer, cleaner, better, with more of the secret opened than locked. I do not feel much confidence in myself as regards to all this, for very few have ever "deserved" eternal life. But with Christ's atonement, and him going on before, I have [hope]. I believe that I shall see him, and know him, and that eternity will be an endless opportunity to consort, that is to be in fellowship with great souls and lesser ones who have entered into the freedom of the heavenly city. It is his forgiveness and grace that give confidence and not merits of my own. But again I say, it's been a great run.[10]

Now that's a person facing death confidently!

The plain teaching of God's Word is that our heavenly hope empowers a joyful life. What does that mean for how we live?

We focus daily on heavenly realities, knowing that this world is not all there is.

We hold earthly things loosely.

We endure suffering courageously.

We serve faithfully.

We resist temptation diligently.

We witness consistently to our heavenly hope.

We face death confidently.

Nothing in this life can compare with heaven. When we think about it clearly, with the mind of Christ, we see how often we are deceived. E. M. Bounds writes:

It was the all engrossing question of the young man who came to Jesus, "What shall I do that I may inherit eternal life?" How attractive and charmful this life! What a divine gift is this life! Yet, it is bounded by the cradle, the symbol of helplessness and want, and by death, the impersonation of all that is dark, painful, and terrific. Enfeebled by disease, hampered by sickness, and marred by sore distress, with severe struggles, sad disappointments, yet to it we cling, for it we toil, and at last surrender it only in a despairing or triumphant struggle.

But eternal life involves the untold, unimagined and fadeless glories of heaven! What measureless wealth! What deathless raptures! What glorious intoxication! No description dare attempt its picture! The most exalted strains of music would be discord to the harmony of heaven and all brightest visions would turn into darkest midnight! All summer suns would chill like the ice of December when contrasted with the splendor of its nightless day. The most gifted, exalted and sweetest poetry of earth would be but dull prose in heaven. What is eternal life? Who can dream or imagine that life? Heaven has it! Heaven holds it! as the surprise of the saints as they leave earth and pass through the gates of the celestial city.[11]

So I close this book with a question: Is heaven in your future? I invite you to say to Jesus Christ, for the first time or as a reaffirmation, "Lord, I believe in you, and I want to live with you forever." Live in the hope of heaven and the hope of eternal life. Get on Jesus' shoulders, and one day you will cross that thunderous cataract of death and come safely, joyfully, to the Other Side.

NOTES

1. C. S. Lewis, *Mere Christianity* (New York: Macmillan Publishing Co., Inc., 1943), 118-119.

2. Steven Covey, *The 7 Habits of Highly Effective People* (New York: Simon & Schuster, 1989), 98.

3. E. M. Bounds, *Heaven: A Place, a City, a Home* (Grand Rapids: Baker Book House, 1975), 128.

4. Jeremy Taylor, *The Rule and Exercises of Holy Living and the Rule and Exercises of Holy Dying,* compiled by Roger L. Roberts (Wilton, Conn.: Morehouse-Barlow Co., Inc., 1981), 34.

5. David Augsburger, *The Freedom of Forgiveness* (Chicago: Moody Press, 1970), 37–38.

6. Gary Provost, "Joe McGinniss, Controlling the Hysteria, Borrowing the Pain, Writing," *Reader's Digest,* (September 1982): 25.

7. E. T. Thompson, "The Sermon on the Mount," in *Sermon on the Mount: Revised Edition,* by Clarence Jordan (Valley Forge: Judson Press, 1970), 39.

8. James S. Hewitt, *Illustrations Unlimited* (Wheaton, Ill.: Tyndale House Publishers, Inc., 1988), 52.

9. Taylor, *The Rule and Exercises of Holy Living and the Rule and Exercises of Holy Dying*, 52.

10. Hewitt, *Illustrations Unlimited*, 150.

11. Bounds, *Heaven: A Place, a City, a Home*, 69–70.

ABOUT THE AUTHOR

Dr. Douglas J. Rumford has pastored congregations for over twenty-one years, most recently as senior pastor of First Presbyterian Church, Fresno, California. He previously served congregations in Old Greenwich, Connecticut, and Fairfield, Connecticut. Now acquisitions director for nonfiction books at Tyndale House Publishers, Doug continues to speak frequently at conferences and churches.

Doug is the author of several books, including *Soul-Shaping* and *Questions God Asks, Questions Satan Asks,* both published by Tyndale House. Doug has also written a number of articles for such publications as *New Man* magazine, *Moody* magazine, *Christianity Today,* and *Leadership* journal.

Doug received his doctor of ministry degree from Fuller Theological Seminary. He earned his master of divinity degree from Gordon-Conwell Theological Seminary, graduating *summa cum laude* as valedictorian of his class, and a bachelor of arts degree from Miami University, Oxford, Ohio.

Doug and his wife, Sarah, have been married twenty-five years and have four children. Doug's goal in ministry is to touch hearts and minds with the truth, grace and power of God: "As I serve Jesus Christ, my greatest joy is bringing ideas to life that can change lives."